EXPLORING A WESLEYAN THEOLOGY

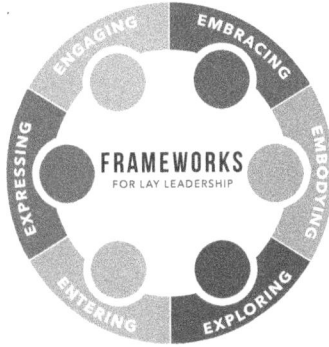

FRAMEWORKS
FOR LAY LEADERSHIP

Rob A. Fringer, series editor

EXPLORING A WESLEYAN THEOLOGY

David B. McEwan

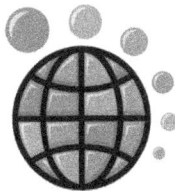

Global Nazarene Publications

ISBN 978-1-56344-869-0

Global Nazarene Publication
Lenexa, Kansas (USA)

TABLE OF CONTENTS

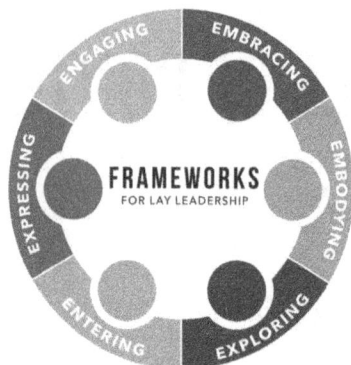

Scripture tells us that believers are "a royal priesthood" (1 Peter 2:9). This means that all Christians, in one form or another, are called into places of ministry and leadership. Not only is this a great privilege, it is also a great responsibility. Men and women desiring to serve in church leadership in some capacity undergo basic training to assure that they understand the foundations of the Christian faith and of our Nazarene identity. This includes a deepening knowledge and appreciation of Scripture, Theology, Ministry, Mission, History, and Holiness. *Frameworks for Lay Leadership* is a series of six books designed to do just that—equip lay leaders for ministry in the Church, whether local, district, or general. These books have the greatest impact when they are read, processed, applied, and contextualised in partnership with a qualified mentor.

Welcome to this journey of transformation!

ENGAGING THE STORY OF GOD
EXPLORING A WESLEYAN THEOLOGY
EMBODYING A THEOLOGY OF MINISTRY AND LEADERSHIP
ENTERING THE MISSION OF GOD
EXPRESSING A NAZARENE IDENTITY
EMBRACING A DOCTRINE OF HOLINESS

CHAPTER 1

JOHN WESLEY AS A THEOLOGIAN

Many Christians regard the study of theology as something that is done by college academics, with little connection to their personal relationship with Christ or life in their local church. Nothing could be further from the truth. To be a Christian is to be a theologian because even confessing that Jesus is Lord is making a theological statement. The question is whether or not our theology is soundly based in Scripture and the heritage of the people of God. The goal of this booklet is to help us anchor our personal and community life on a solid foundation that is faithful to the Gospel of Christ and the Christian community over the centuries.

The Church of the Nazarene traces its roots back to the New Testament church and the theological deposit contained in the ecumenical creeds of the first five centuries. It traces its Protestant and evangelical heritage to the ministry and writings of John Wesley and his brother Charles during the 18th century revival that led to the establishment of the Methodist church and the range of denominations that flowed from it. We self-identify as a member of the Wesleyan church family, and our theological framework is profoundly Wesleyan.[1]

In the early church, the role of the theologian was not to develop a theological system and defend it at an academic level. Instead it was to nurture and shape a genuinely Christian worldview to frame both temperament and practice. The primary task was not to write systematic theology or apologetics, but to provide practical and pastoral tools for personal and community formation.[2] John Wesley stands in this tradition. He drew his theological resources from the early Church, his own Church of England, and the developing Methodist movement. His understanding of God and the people God created is remarkably consistent over his whole ministry. It is centred in love and relationships, rather than the intellectual understanding of facts about God, humans, and the process of salvation. This makes the heart and transforming relationship central to his theologising, rather than logical systems and precise doctrinal statements. It is for this reason that membership in the Church of the Nazarene requires "only such avowals of belief as are *essential* to Christian experience."[3] We believe:

- In one God—the Father, Son, and Holy Spirit.

- The Old and New Testament Scriptures, given by plenary inspiration, contain all truth necessary to faith and Christian living.

- Human beings are born with a fallen nature, and are, therefore, inclined to evil, and that continually.

- The finally impenitent are hopelessly and eternally lost.

- The atonement through Jesus Christ is for the whole human race; and that whosoever repents and believes on the Lord Jesus Christ is justified and regenerated and saved from the dominion of sin.

- That believers are to be sanctified wholly, subsequent to regeneration, through faith in the Lord Jesus Christ.

- The Holy Spirit bears witness to the new birth, and also to the entire sanctification of believers.

- Our Lord will return, the dead will be raised, and the final judgment will take place.[4]

This emphasises that our theology has an essential, practical focus; it is anchored in and supportive of the ministry of the church, both to its own people and to the wider community. We focus on our relationship with God, with other people, and the rest of the creation, not merely on an intellectual grasp of doctrines.

The Nature of Theology

Christianity is not just about feelings and morals; there is a message to be proclaimed and accepted. The question we ask all candidates for baptism is "Do you believe...?" and that means there are things to be affirmed if we are to be faithful followers of Jesus Christ. Some of these are regarded as essential—what we call dogma—and are summarised in the great creeds of the Church: the Apostles' Creed (origins are in the 2nd century), Nicene Creed (AD 381), Chalcedonian Creed (AD 451), and the Athanasian Creed (AD 500). Of these, the Apostles' Creed and the Nicene Creed are the most commonly confessed, with the latter being the truly ecumenical creed upheld by every orthodox, Christian tradition. Derived from these, and often expanded, are the various confessions which tend to be more historically and culturally bound, seeking to engage more specifically with the questions of the day in which they were originally drafted. For example, the Augsburg Confession (AD 1530) for Lutherans and the Westminster Confession (AD 1646) for several Reformed churches. Many evangelical churches, including the Church of the Nazarene, have "Articles of Faith" which are more specifically related to their denomination. As an Anglican, Wesley followed a non-dogmatic approach to Christianity that discouraged the construction of such confessions and systematic treatises. Instead, he emphasised the centrality of the community at worship, united by a common liturgy. He believed that the main emphasis was to be on love and relationship—in terms of defining both the essential nature of God and human beings. The implication is that salvation is understood within a framework of relationship between the divine Lover and the human beloved, which focuses on the "heart," rather than a framework of laws between a Sovereign and a subject, which focuses on an intellectual knowledge of content and application.

If "true religion"—a phrase often used by Wesley—is a matter of the heart and relationship, then the ministry of the Holy Spirit is central to the initiation, development, and consummation of the life of faith in both personal and community experience. The person who is impacted by the ministry of the Holy Spirit could not know this other than by personal experience—what we call the witness of the Spirit. The work of the Spirit impacts the entire person and not just the mind. The Spirit may work more particularly on the understanding to open or enlighten it; the Spirit may work on the will and affections, withdrawing us from evil and inclining us to good. Wesley realised the need for various safeguards in theologising, but these safeguards had to be such that they did not deny or stifle the direct work of the Spirit in the heart. It is here that his concept of "the means of grace" becomes critical. These are the sources and practices that God uses to instruct and guide people in their spiritual life. Of particular importance for Wesley are prayer and searching the Scriptures (which implies reading, hearing, and meditating on them). In both prayer and searching the Scriptures, Wesley emphasised that we need to use both our personal reasoning and experience, as well as that of the church community, if we are to live faithfully for Christ. Practically, Wesley makes Scripture of first importance (as all Protestants do) in contradistinction to Roman Catholicism's emphasis on the place of tradition or the Enlightenment thinkers who elevated reason to that place. In terms of sequence, Wesley said, "We prove the doctrines we preach by Scripture and reason; and, if needed, by antiquity."[5]

QUESTIONS FOR REFLECTION

1. Have you ever thought of yourself as a theologian? Why or why not?

2. What are some of the practical implications for every Christian being a theologian?

3. What difference does it make for inter-church relationships if we focus on the centrality of loving relationships rather than the mastery of doctrine?

CHAPTER 2

THE DOCTRINE OF GOD

WE BELIEVE
In one God—the Father, Son, and Holy Spirit

The Doctrine of God is at the centre of our theological framework, and distortions here have profound consequences. It covers both the nature of God and God's relationship to all of creation—including human beings. Most heresies stem from a faulty understanding of the doctrine of God. Within orthodox Christianity, different perspectives influence our understanding of such things as how God provides salvation through Christ. At the heart of John Wesley's theological understanding was the claim that the essential nature of God is love, and this is expressed relationally within the triune Godhead of Father, Son, and Holy Spirit. The content of this love is defined by God's nature and activities, particularly as they are revealed to us in the person and work of Jesus Christ. It is this personal, relational knowledge of God that makes possible a true knowledge of his nature and character. We experience God as *holy love*, and all his attributes need to be interpreted as expressions of that central reality. For example, Wesleyans define God's sovereignty as the sovereignty of love (enabling all to respond while not forcing a particular response), rather than naked power. The Augustinian/Lutheran/Reformed position sees love as a manifestation of his will (and so love for the "elect"), whereas Wesleyans see it as a manifestation of his nature (love for "all"), with the offer of salvation extended to every person (though not all will accept). We will explore this further when we examine our understanding of salvation.

God's holiness is not primarily a moral attribute (it is not perfect goodness), but signifies his absolute otherness that distinguishes the Creator from his creation. This makes it a qualitative difference and not a quantitative one and avoids seeing God existing only to serve our interests or for our benefit. It prohibits us from interpreting God's character and nature in complete continuity with human categories. It affirms that God loves us because he wants to, not because he needs us. His love is a pure, unbiased love for our well-being and is not tied in any way to our obedience or self-worth. It also guards against misinterpreting sin simply in a moralistic way and thus losing its distinctively religious character.

Biblical Teaching

In the Old Testament, God is presented as the Living God who acts in human history and seeks relationships with all people. He is also the Holy God, and as such he alone is worthy of worship, calling us to an exclusive relationship that requires that we be a holy people. The people of Israel were monotheistic (belief that only one God exists), rather than henotheistic (belief in many gods while worshipping only one). The Christian church accepted the Old Testament as an authentic self-revelation of God, but they had to go beyond it because of the deeper revelation received in Jesus Christ. It was this revelation and the new experience of God that forced the early church to develop a Trinitarian understanding of God. The church tried both unitarian and binitarian models, but neither view found acceptance since they did not do full justice either to the witness of the New Testament or their own experience of God. Certainly, the doctrine of the Trinity is not explicitly taught in Scripture; however, it is clearly implicit. The Old Testament was monotheistic (Exodus 20:2-4; Deuteronomy 6:4-5) and this same belief is found in the New Testament (Matthew 23:37; James 2:19; 1 Timothy 2:5-6; 1 Corinthians 8:4, 6). We also have clear, biblical evidence for the divinity of the Father (1 Corinthian 8:4, 6; 1 Timothy 2:5-6; Matthew

6:26, 30, 31-32; 19:23-26; 27:46; Mark 12:17, 24-27). The divinity of Jesus is revealed in such passages as Philippians 2:5-11 (especially verse six, where "form" indicates the genuine nature of a thing) and Hebrews 1. There are clear indications of Jesus's own self-consciousness in passages like Mark 2:8-10; Matthew 12:28; 19:14, 24; 21:31, 43; 25:31; 24:30; 26:63-65; John 19:28; 20:28. The divinity of the Spirit is seen in Matthew 28:19; John 3:8; John 16:8-11; Acts 5:3-4; 1 Corinthians 3:16-17 with 6:19-20; 1 Corinthians 12:4-11; 2 Corinthians 13:14; and 1 Peter 1:2. There are a few refences in the New Testament that seem to indicate a triune understanding, such as Matthew 28:19-20; 2 Corinthians 13:14 and 1 Thessalonians 1:2-5; but there are many passages that are triadic by inference.

Historically, long before the *dogma* of the Trinity, was the Church's *experience* of the Trinity. In Romans 8:15 and Galatians 4:6 the church testified to the witness of the Spirit and the privilege of being a child of God through Jesus Christ, highlighting the Trinitarian structure of Christian experience. Our belief comes from sustained and critical reflection on the pattern of the divine activity revealed in Scripture and continued in Christian experience. It took the church several centuries to settle on an acceptable theology of the Trinity. In the Eastern church, the Cappadocian Fathers (three theologians writing in the 4th century) explained the Triune God as "being-in-communion." The three Persons cannot be conceived to be or to act separately. One cannot sever the Spirit from Christ, who is the only mediator of creation, nor can you sever either of them from the Father, so there is only *one* God in *being*. This is not a mathematical oneness but a oneness consisting in the inseparable eternal relation of Father, Son, and Spirit. From now on, the word "God" was to be understood in a totally different way. God *is* no more than what the Father, Son, and Spirit give to and receive from each other in the inseparable communion that is the outcome of their love; there is no *being* of God other than this dynamic of persons in an eternal relation. Augustine (5th century) tended to focus on the unity of the Godhead (the "One" God) and this profoundly influenced western Christianity and the eventual rise of the notion of the individual before

God. However, it was Augustine who emphasised the place of love in the divine life and therefore in the God-human relationship. This beautifully complements the Cappadocian's social analogy of the Trinity and returns the focus to loving relationships as the heart of personhood.

QUESTIONS FOR REFLECTION

1. Why is our understanding of the nature of God so important for shaping the rest of our theology?

2. Read through some of the passages listed in this section about the Trinity. What do you learn?

3. Is the doctrine of the Trinity central to our faith or is it something we can ignore? What difference does it make to our personal and community life?

CHAPTER 3

THE DOCTRINE OF SCRIPTURE

WE BELIEVE
The Old and New Testament Scriptures, given by plenary inspiration, contain all truth necessary to faith and Christian living

The unique strength of Wesley's theological method was the recognition, explanation, and application of the sources of tradition and experience as essential components in reading, understanding, and applying (by using human reason) the primary religious source of Scripture, under the guidance of the Holy Spirit. Scripture is foundational, and the other elements enable the church to organise, illumine, and apply Scripture in theological reflection and practice. They do not add to biblical truth but confirm and understand it. The Bible requires explanation beyond what is available in its words alone, so we must make use of interpretative motifs provided by tradition, enabled through reason, and confirmed by knowledge gained from experience (personal and community). Scripture is a safeguard against irresponsible appeals to enthusiastic, mystical, or other subjective experiences. Wesley believed that truth is experimental—Christian beliefs must ultimately be capable of proof in personal and community experience. We begin with our preunderstanding and what is presented for integration into our present knowledge or its transformation; experience then calls this into question and we must decide what to retain, reuse, or reject. The mature Wesley consciously sought to guide this by Scripture as enlightened by reason, experience, and tradition under the illuminating work of the Holy Spirit.

Scripture

For Wesleyans, the primary authority is the Christ himself (the Living Word), and everything else is only authoritative to the degree it adequately witnesses to the Lord himself. The key element here is that God's self-disclosure takes place primarily in history and this involves questions of *facticity, meaning, significance,* and *application.* History gives us the eyewitnesses and the reports of eyewitnesses to Jesus Christ. The Scripture is the primary record and faithful interpretation of salvation history. The Bible is the original document about the events and their meaning on which the Church is founded. It exists as a book that can be read and studied, and there are facts associated with it which cannot be ignored and still allow for a faithful interpretation of that text. For example, the Ten Commandments are not the ten suggestions! The decisive difference between agreeing and disagreeing with a speaker and a written text is that in conversation you can ask the other speaker for clarification; a written text cannot answer back or defend itself. We need a living, personal reality to maintain the text's independence, and for us the Holy Spirit is the final defender of the text against its interpreters, in the church or otherwise. The Spirit works through the *community* (the universality of the Church at all times and places), over against any of its individual members or associations. It is the intimate link between the final and full revelation of God in Christ and the Scripture that gives us confidence to believe that it is the foundational source for determining specifically Christian belief and practice. The Scripture is clear on all essential points regarding our salvation, and it is this focus on the salvation story that is the main guide to our interpretation and application of the text.

The authority of the Bible for us is not settled by the authority of the church nor by what the text itself claims, otherwise the Book of Mormon is just as authoritative as the Bible. It is settled by the *internal testimony of the Holy Spirit*. This position was strongly upheld by Martin Luther and John Calvin, as well as by John Wesley. The inspiration of the original writers through the work of the Spirit is intimately linked to the illuminating work of the same Spirit who opens our hearts and minds to see and receive the truth being expressed. This internal witness of the Spirit and the transformation of present Christian lives (the external witness of the Spirit) is the strongest evidence for the truth of biblical revelation. For Wesleyans, the authority of Scripture is based on its sufficiency for bringing about a transforming relationship with God. It is possible to have an authentic experience of God without a full grasp of all the theological implications of the faith, and this allows for growth in personal experience as our knowledge increases through study and reflection on Scripture. In the end, our attitude to God determines our attitude to his Word; it is not a matter of our capacity but our unwillingness to understand ("I don't understand because I won't understand").

Tradition

Tradition is the link that tries to ensure that what we have received from those coming before us in the church is faithfully passed on to others. Both dimensions are important as we wrestle with coming to a sound knowledge of the historical events (facts), their interpretation (meaning), significance and application in our own day. Wesley did not appeal to Christian tradition as a whole; his focus was the Early Church (particularly the first three centuries) and the Anglican standards. He focused more on the people and their witness (especially the Eastern Fathers) than the creeds. He saw them as people whose lives were to be emulated in the present. As a Protestant, he believed that tradition could never be over Scripture, but it could help us to clarify ambiguous aspects and give specific applications of Scripture's general principles. Wesley used it to refute practices or beliefs he saw as harmful and to defend practices or beliefs he saw as helpful. In tradition, he also found patterns for practices, beliefs, and virtues to be restored. This helped him to demonstrate how his Methodist teachings and practices were in harmony with Scripture even though not prescribed by it. The church must always interpret the faith in contemporary terms, otherwise it becomes a dead faith of interest only to historians. We now have 2,000 years of "contemporary" interpretations to draw upon, and this will continue till the Lord returns. All our denominational "traditions" need to be evaluated by "the tradition" of the early Church to minimise the danger of "canonising" any particular expression of the faith.

Experience

Revelation by definition is communication, and for this to occur the message must both be *given* and *received*. Only with reception can we determine its *significance*. All events (actions or words) are *experienced* by persons, and this makes experience a *medium* of revelation rather than a *source* of revelation. Experience conveys truth, but it does not create it. Wesley was the first to incorporate experience explicitly into a theological worldview (Anglicans had worked with scripture, reason and tradition). As an empiricist, Wesley used both objective knowledge attained through observation and subjective knowledge obtained through inner experience. An essential element of such experience must be the inner witness of the Holy Spirit. Experience was, therefore, a *confirming source* used to verify the theological claims of Scripture. It was an experimental verification within life itself (personal and community transformation) that we have read, interpreted, and applied the Scripture correctly. For Wesleyans, the content (*substance*) of doctrine is derived from Scripture, but the practical application (*circumstance*) is derived from experience. It is important to note that it was community experience that was essential (the *public* character of the experience) and not private experience. The work of the Spirit in personal and community life must always be checked and given guidance by the Word. Since God is never self-contradictory, what he says (Scripture) and what he does (Spirit) are always in agreement. This is the test as to whether an "experience" is truly Christian. Wesley was insistent that the work of the Spirit and the Scriptural record were normative for both personal and community experience, and this minimised the danger of the Christian becoming mired in purely mystical and subjective experiences. A genuine encounter with the Spirit bears scriptural fruit that can be validated in life by an observer's appeal to the test of Scripture and reason.

The major appeal by Wesley to personal and community experience was not for formulating or testing doctrinal claims, but to provide the assurance that empowers us for Christian living (to be able "to love" we must first have "experienced" love). This "experience" was not an individual's feelings on a matter, but an analysis of the objective realities of their Christian life and testimony. Christian doctrine and doctrinal discernment had to prove true in personal and community life over time (the longer the better). For Wesley, wisdom was acquired through life in community and not by immediate spiritual sensation. The gathering and sharing of personal and community witness was a central task of theology, and it provided a public evidence of the truth of core Christian teachings. Wesleyans believe that it was the same self-revealing God being encountered through Scripture, tradition, and experience, when each of these was rightly and rationally utilised. It is lived experience that clarifies the claims found in Scripture or tradition; it tests the possible interpretations of Scripture or tradition and helps us to correlate apparently disparate claims within these sources. Christian experience suggests and tests contextual applications of the biblical material and helps us to address doctrinal and practical issues not clearly addressed in Scripture or tradition. It makes use of the pastoral wisdom that is nurtured by practical testing in the daily corporate life of the Christian community and is enriched by conferring broadly with the experience of others. So, Scripture teaches what should be expected, and experience teaches it was fulfilled in the lives of people. However, where Scripture and experience diverge, the former is trustworthy and the latter untrustworthy. Experience is how we appropriate the authority of Scripture, not the authority itself.

Reason

Reason is the integrating medium between Scripture, tradition, and experience, as well as a creative means of addressing issues neither commanded nor forbidden by Scripture. It is the most used criterion for Wesley after Scripture, as he usually conjoins Scripture and reason rather than Scripture alone. It helps us to interpret, understand, and respond to the claims of revelation but is not an independent source for theology nor can it demonstrate the truths of Christianity. Scripture is always the primary resource and norm for religious knowledge, but reason is essential to understand and communicate it to others. It has a different kind of authority than the other three: each of them is a resource from which to draw data, whereas reason *processes* the data from these sources. It should always be used in conversation with others (both the living and those now dead who have left us records); this underlines the vital place of "Christian conference" for the church as well as the individual Christian. Reason can discover absurdities in reading the Bible with a wooden literalism or where Scripture appears to contradict itself. It is equally important for bridging the gap between the general rule or principle in Scripture and the contemporary situation. In all of this, we need the ministry of the Spirit to enlighten and correct reason.

QUESTIONS FOR REFLECTION

1. How would you respond to a Christian who claims that all we ever need to read is the Bible?

2. Describe the role of the Holy Spirit in the process of inspiring the Bible and then our reading of it.

3. What happens to the church when we neglect its history? How concerned should we be by the rejection of tradition and an overvaluing of contemporary experience?

4. Are feelings a safe guide to our spiritual life? What tends to happen if we live simply by how we feel?

5. If reason is important, how do we help people to think wisely and well?

CHAPTER 4

THE DOCTRINE OF SIN

WE BELIEVE
Human beings are born with a fallen nature, and are, therefore, inclined to evil, and that continually.

The beginning point for Wesleyans is not what went wrong with God's creation but how it was in the beginning—what sort of world did God originally create? In terms of humanity, this has to do with the claim that we were made in "the image of God." There are only three passages in the Old Testament that provide explicit teaching about the "image of God" (Genesis 1:26-28; 5:1-5; 9:1-7), whereas the theme is more common in the New Testament, particularly in the context of the image damaged by sin and restored through Christ's redemptive work (1 Corinthians 11:7; James 3:9; see also Romans 8:29; 2 Corinthians 3:18; Ephesians 4:23-24; Colossians 3:10). This also raises questions about the humanity of Jesus Christ, and its relationship to our humanity (see for example John 13:15; Romans 15:5; 2 Corinthians 10:1; Philippians 2:5; Colossians 3:13), which we will return to later. The present human reality is then introduced in Genesis 3—the first sin and its consequences. This raises the issues of humanity as God intended versus humanity as it now exists.

The Relationship between God and Humankind

The Scripture account begins with a strong hint at God's own relational character: "Let *us* make man in *our* image" (Genesis 1.26), an allusion greatly expanded in the Trinitarian theology of the New Testament. In Trinitarian theology persons are defined by being related to another who is *different*. It is striking that the Genesis "image of God" passages refer in each case to the relationship between God and Adam in the sense of humankind, explicitly referring in each case to the diversity of his creation in making male and female (cf. Genesis 1:27; 5:2; 9:6-7). The love that exists between the Father, Son, and Holy Spirit is to be reflected in the love displayed in human relationships. It is "person-in-relation-to-God" and never "person-in-relation-to-themselves." We are in the image of God, and it is not the image of God in us. It is not a natural possession but a spiritual one; it is not "an extension of the divine in us" or a "divine spark" in us, but a relationship within which we stand. We find our true being in loving relationships. Therefore, from a Wesleyan standpoint, we cannot define "person" in reductionist, individualistic terms. The older individualism grew out of a belief in the objectivity of God—the Creator of natural and moral law, who also created individuals with rights to life, liberty, and the pursuit of happiness. Religion was then a means towards self-realisation.

The focus of the creation narrative is the relationship between the Creator and the human creature, and this relationship is essentially defined by love.[6] This was no isolated reference, but lies at the heart of Wesley's whole theological framework:

> For to this end was man created, to love God; and to this end alone, even to love the Lord his God with all his heart, and soul, and mind, and strength. But love is the very image of God: it is the brightness of his glory. By love, man is not only made like God, but in some sense one with him. He "dwelleth in God, and God in him;" and "he that is thus joined to the Lord is one spirit."[7]

For Wesley, it is love that is the essence of the life of the Triune God and it is this same quality that lies at the heart of being human—both in terms of relationship with God and with the neighbour. The focus on the essential nature of God as love is not unique to Wesley and several recent books emphasise its rich heritage in the theology of the church, especially the contributions of Augustine and Thomas Aquinas.

Human Freedom

The image of God as created in love requires the reality of human freedom; human beings as created were self-determined in their decisions, though they may well be influenced by a whole range of factors. We are not absolutely free as such; freedom is not an ability, capacity, quality that is possessed, but a *relationship* that is lived. The structure of the Genesis account very carefully shows us there was no necessity for sin, and it is not inherent to the human situation. We cannot be free for God, unless we can also be free from God. Wesley believed that God freely made us in love and for love, so we had to be capable of freely returning the love received, which requires the ability to exercise genuine choice. A love that is compelled through original design, or by simple coercion from a greater power, would not be love at all—it would reduce us to robots or to puppets. We were given liberty (freedom) to keep or change this first estate, with no compulsion from God or any other being. Wesley is adamant that without the power to choose the good and refuse what was not, a genuinely loving relationship was impossible.

> Without this both the will and the understanding would have been utterly useless. Indeed without liberty man had been so far from being a *free agent* that he could have been no *agent* at all. For every *unfree being* is purely passive, not active in any degree. … He that is not free is not an agent, but a patient [that is, one acted upon].[8]

It is the genuine power of choice that enables us to be held accountable for those choices: "There is no virtue but where an intelligent being knows, loves, and chooses what is good; nor is there any vice but where such a being knows, loves, and chooses what is evil."[9] God gave us the freedom to choose either good or evil, and therefore to be accountable and responsible for those choices and their outcomes. That meant that humanity had to face some form of clear test, a situation that provided an alternate choice; otherwise it was not real liberty (which is the power of contrary choice).[10] Wesley believed that the original humans would not have chosen evil knowing it to be such, "But it cannot be doubted he might mistake evil for good. He was not infallible."[11] Humanity was not created knowing all things (that would make us divine), so ignorance is not in itself evil, though it may lead to evil if wrong choices are made. In reflecting upon Genesis 2:17 and the command to not eat the fruit from the tree of the knowledge of good and evil, Wesley saw God providing a clear test of the quality of the relationship that was unambiguous: continue to trust me and do not eat this fruit and live; do not trust me, eat this fruit and die. This perfect existence came to an end when Adam and Eve succumbed to the temptation to doubt God's love and goodness, ceased to trust him, and ate the forbidden fruit. The critical issue here is not the extent of human knowledge, but the depth of human trust. Lacking omniscience (the ability to know all things), humanity either had to trust God for those areas of life that were not understood and obey based on trust alone, or refuse to trust and try and find answers for themselves. As finite creatures, we will never be equal to the Creator, but the temptation lies at the point of the possibility of knowing, doing, being more than we are now on our own terms rather than God's. If we doubt God's love and goodness, then we may be persuaded that our best option is to take matters into our own hands and cross the boundary the Creator put in place for our well-being and safety, believing that the boundary is in fact a restriction on our freedom rather than its guarantee.

Humanity and Sin: The Doctrine of Original Sin in Wesley

Humanity fell from their original created state through unbelief by not continuing to trust God, his goodness and love. Since we were created as dependent creatures and all we have is from God, through our own choice we turned from God, lost the indwelling presence of the Holy Spirit, and became self-centred, selfish, and self-willed. Being deprived of the Spirit, we became "depraved" (the first sin is the cause, and depravity is the effect). This impacts every area of our life because of our alienation from God. While Wesley does refer to original sin in his writings, his preferred term is "inbeing sin" and it is best understood in terms of the loss of loving relationship with God, with the neighbour, and the rest of creation. This arises from the corruption of our nature due to the loss of the indwelling Spirit, and it is this corruption that leads to the destruction of our relationships unless we respond positively to the work of God's prevenient grace (see later for a further explanation of this). Because of Adam's sin, death (spiritual, temporal, and eternal) came upon the entire race; guilt attaches to the depravity of our hearts and our sinful inclinations, yet only personal guilt, deriving from our own actual sins, leads to eternal death. Wesleyan theologians generally see a key distinction between personal blameworthiness and liability to penalty; while actual, personal sin has both, original sin carries only the latter as it was not our conscious choice and therefore cannot carry culpability. Wesley (based on his Notes on Romans 5) says since we are not responsible for inbeing sin, we are not punished with eternal death for this alone (due to prevenient grace).[12] The doctrine of original sin is theology's way of affirming the universality of sin.

Does it affirm we all *must* sin or that we all *do* sin? The Christian paradox affirms that sin is both inevitable and volitional, and this paradox cannot be resolved without loss to orthodox theology. Some resolved the paradox by denying original sin (we are all our own "Adam"), while extreme Calvinism resolved the paradox by making it inevitable to the exclusion of our personal choice. Wesleyanism affirms that sin is not an essential element of human nature as created; yet, in practice, we all do sin (Romans 3:23). Theologically it underscores two fundamental truths. Firstly, every individual human being is now a "sinner" before God. For Wesley, total depravity refers to its extent because it infects every area of our life and therefore everything we do, say, or think is impacted. Actual sin is always an expression of original sin. Secondly, it indicates a solidarity in sin—the whole human race is equally damaged.

Wesley's focus is much more on the answer to the problem (salvation), than to its source and origin. He was convinced that inbeing sin lies further back than our conscious choice; it is part of the world before our own birth and in some way, it is related to what happened in Adam.

Here we must note that Wesley's understanding of the doctrine of salvation and prevenient grace led him to affirm that all may recover what was lost in Adam. Therefore, God cannot be charged with injustice in punishing us for Adam's sin. On the other hand, Calvinism uses the doctrine of predestination and election to uphold God's justice: justice condemns the whole race and elective mercy spares some, but the rest of humanity cannot complain since they only receive what they deserved. Wesley believed God wills to save all; that prevenient grace is given to all so that salvation is a genuine possibility for all, and this grace is the source of all good in human beings (the activity of the conscience). No one sins because they have no grace, but all sin because they do not use the grace they have. Some are not saved because they choose not to be— thus God's justice is upheld.

A Right Conception of Sin

In Wesleyan thought, sin is not an abstract concept and it does not exist independently of us; it is not a "thing" or a quality attached to our being, but the moral condition of a personal being. Good and evil are personal terms and so we properly refer to "the human sinner." In the Bible, it is perhaps best understood as a violation of a covenant relationship. The pivotal passages are Genesis 1–11 (where the standard terms for sin are minimal) and Romans 1–3. In Romans 3:23 "missing the mark" is clearly identified as "falling short of the glory of God" and in the New Testament "glory" is usually a synonym for "image" (see 1 Corinthians 11:7; 2 Corinthians 3:18).

It is important to understand what is being conveyed to us in the Genesis creation account. It is easy to see the human as complete and God as external, with the presence of the Spirit internally only required after the Fall. However, Genesis 2:7, with its reference to the "breath" (Spirit) of God, as well as the balance of Scripture, reminds us that to be human at all means to be indwelt by the Spirit of God. It was not merely an external relationship but an internal relationship from the very beginning, and the person was totally dependent on the ministry of the Spirit as an essential element of "creaturehood."

Sin is to act out of the "self" rather than the Spirit; it is a turning away from God's gracious presence and a refusal to continue to participate in the fullness of God's love. It is a religious category and has meaning only in terms of our relationship to God, and any other setting perverts the truth (justice and crime, ethics and good/evil, psychology and normal/abnormal are valid, but none of them are "sin"). Sin does have an ethical component, but this is not its essence.

Our understanding of the nature of sin controls our understanding of holiness:

- if sin is a violation of law (behaviour)…
    …holiness is flawless behaviour

- if sin is a series of acts…
    …holiness is a pattern of forgiveness

- if sin a rational exercise…
    …holiness is orthodoxy

If sin is essentially a turning from God, perverted love, a violation of covenant relationship, then holiness is orienting the whole person to God and a genuinely restored relationship. Four major frameworks for understanding the essential nature of sin are common:

1. *Sin as unbelief.* This is not primarily an intellectual category or the very normal human "doubt;" it is a wilful lack of trust and confidence in God (Romans 14:23); a rejection of God's goodness and love, and his Lordship as Creator

2. *Sin as egocentricity and pride.* To be self-sovereign rather than under God's sovereignty. This is a delusion and lies at the heart of idolatry (see Romans 1:18ff and the refusal to worship God as God).

3. *Sin as disobedience.* For Wesley, "sin properly so-called" is a "voluntary transgression of a known law."[13] This is based on 1 John 3:4: "sin is lawlessness"—an attitude, a mindset that declares we are free from legitimate constraints, leading to anarchy and rebellion. It is to this inner rebellion that Wesley's definition points, not the "acts" as such, but the motivation that lies behind them.

4. *Sin as sensuality.* Seeking our own gratification (egocentric); self-love.

It is important to see that there is also a social dimension to sin. The biblical concept is seen in Adam and Christ as "corporate persons" (Romans 5:12-21). All of us are both individuals and members of society. We are conditioned by its realities and function within its context (political, vocational, moral, intellectual, educational, family, geography, race, culture). Our fallen world is now under the control of Satan directly or indirectly, and evil has a status apart from and independent of any individual human will, identified in Scripture as "the world." While "the world" in Scripture can refer to the planet, the human race, or the current human population, it can also refer to a spiritual force totally opposed to God. It is a whole chaotic system of spiritual forces that are the very embodiment of evil and corrupt all under its influence. We are caught up in this simply by being alive. With our human inclination to develop idolatries, it is often difficult to recognise social sin simply because we are not inclined to regard the consequences of personal involvement in things where we do not have an active choice. Membership in the group may have coloured our perception of reality and we may not see group selfishness because of our own individual selfishness. Our excesses are less obvious to us because of the group we belong to and the further removed we are from the actual evil, the less real it seems. We can be involved by financial involvement (taxes, dues, shares, and purchases), direct approval (voting), or tacit consent (not disagreeing or registering opposition).

QUESTIONS FOR REFLECTION

1. What are the consequences of an overly-individualistic understanding of the Christian faith?

2. How would you explain the relationship of love and freedom? How does this affect the personal and community consequences of our choices?

3. How would you describe the relationship between the first sin recorded in Genesis 3 and the way we live before we come to faith in Christ?

4. The word "sin" is rarely used outside of the church; how would you explain its reality to a non-Christian?

5. What is the connection between my personal sin and the present state of the world as a whole?

CHAPTER 5

THE DOCTRINE OF SALVATION

WE BELIEVE
The atonement through Jesus Christ is for the whole human race; and that whosoever repents and believes on the Lord Jesus Christ is justified and regenerated and saved from the dominion of sin

There is no ecumenical unifying creedal statement on the basic meaning of the atonement; all orthodox creeds confess Jesus as Saviour, but none say what must be believed about *how* he saves—and on this point diversity is greater than uniformity amongst key Christian theologians. The basic understanding is found in the Bible, though it gives us a rich diversity of images and metaphors. In the New Testament, we are told that it is Christ's life, death, and resurrection that is the sole basis for the salvation of humanity through the grace and mercy of God. It is an objective provision for reconciliation between God and humanity through the person and work of Jesus Christ, making possible forgiveness and transformation of all those who believe and trust in him. The language of *sacrifice, substitution,* and *reconciliation* is widespread.

New Testament Images of Christ's Work

The New Testament uses many figures of speech for the Atonement and from these we then try to "construct" a systematic theology. Whatever the language used, it is clearly linked with Christ's death on the cross as the "Suffering Servant" (see Isaiah 40—55) and the important role of the teaching at the Last Supper: Matthew 26:28—Exodus and Passover motifs; the "victory" of God (Colossians 2:15; Ephesians 4:8); the "power" of the Servant in weakness (1 Corinthians 1:20-31; Isaiah 42:6; 49:8). Sacrificial language is used in both the Old and New Testaments to establish covenant relations (Genesis 15; Exodus 24) and to maintain covenant relations (1 Corinthians 5:5; 15:23). A covenant is person-oriented and not thing-oriented (like a contract); the breaking of a covenant is not always clear-cut because it involves personal intimacy and not simply a point on a contract. Doctrinally, all the models of the atonement that we derive from these and similar passages have strengths and weaknesses. From a Wesleyan framework, we must measure each model against the clear biblical portrayal of God as "holy love." Holiness prevents us overlooking or failing to deal conclusively with the question of sin, and love prevents us from insisting on some satisfaction of abstract justice before God is willing to forgive or justify the sinner. Our doctrine of sin means there must be an interpersonal dimension to reconciliation; atonement cannot simply deal with the sin but not the sinner. Our model of the atonement cannot be based on "so much sin = so much penalty to be paid." God does not keep a quantitative record requiring a corresponding price to be paid before forgiveness is possible. This is a critical limitation of understanding sin substantially rather than relationally. The early church Father, Irenaeus, reminds us the focus of salvation lies in the *restoration* to be achieved more than the payment to be made.

Wesley insisted on the *fact* of the atonement, but not on any one explanation. He believed the benefits were always justification, sanctification, and the restoration of the whole creation in glorification. It is the objective ground for Wesley's *optimism of grace* and the unmerited source of prevenient grace. It must faithfully portray both God's work *in* us and *for* us. Since he had no specific formulation, we find him adopting and using others, especially some form of satisfaction theory (that is, the death of Christ in some way satisfies both divine love and divine justice). His practical bent and fondness for scriptural language is seen in his frequent quotations of Philippians 2:8; 2 Corinthians 5:14, 19, 21; 1 John 2:1. He affirmed that Christ's sacrifice was complete and perfect with no further work or repetition needed (John 19:30). The atonement is an offering, a sacrifice, that involves a great price—the death of Christ; neither forgiveness nor justification comes cheaply nor easily. It is a "satisfaction" for the sins of the whole world (1 John 2:2). Romans 3:25-26 showed that God takes sin with the utmost seriousness in the same moment that he forgives it. It is an offence that the ungodly should be spared their punishment, so how can sin be forgiven righteously? The answer is at Calvary where God's love and justice meet—the supreme demonstration of love and the supreme condemnation of sin. Here God is righteous, is seen to be righteous, and at the same moment puts right the unrighteous sinner.

Toward a Wesleyan Model

This section is based on recent work by Nazarene theologian, Thomas Noble, who draws out from Wesley's writings a model of the atonement that avoids many of the problems with some of the other models—especially penal substitution (the belief that Christ paid the penalty for our sins, enabling the guilty sinner to be justly declared innocent).[14] The key is Wesley's use of the threefold office of Christ as *Prophet, Priest,* and *King* (Calvin also works with the three offices, but in a slightly different way). Interpreted soteriologically, the Prophet meets our need of knowledge of God and his will; the Priest enables a right relationship with God; and the King enables freedom from our enslavement to sin.

1. The Prophetic Work of Christ

The prophet declares, "Thus says the Lord" as the agent of God's revelation to his people. In Jesus Christ, we have the perfect revealer of divine truth in both his person and teaching. While the Old Testament prophets *spoke* the word of God, this Prophet *is* the Word of God. Now the Word enters human history by becoming a human being. In so doing, Christ becomes our kinsman-redeemer, who had to be a relative with the resources to redeem the one caught in bondage. The Law of God is simply the embodiment of the very nature of God and expresses how we were always intended to live as people created in his image. Our rebellion means we are no longer able to live as God created us to live. Jesus comes as fully human but with the full resources of his divine nature so that our debt can be fully paid. We are not just saved by Jesus, but saved in Jesus. By nature, we are unable to keep God's law, but Jesus as the perfect human (without sin) keeps the law perfectly; if we are in union with him, then all the power of his resources become our resources. What the law demands, we are now able to do "in Christ."

2. The Priestly Work of Christ

The work of the priest is often regarded as simply offering sacrifices and making intercession on behalf of the people. However, it also embodies the notion of being a "bridge-builder" who connects both God and humanity. The law required a sin-offering to remind us of the objective reality of sin; that it was not just something in our minds. The western (Latin) tradition developed this legal model to affirm the objective reality of the debt we owe to God because of our sin. It was advanced by Calvin and other Reformed theologians into the penal substitutionary model, in which Christ pays the penalty for our sins. Wesleyans have always regarded the category of "punishment" as biblically questionable but the legal model itself is Scriptural, legitimate, and necessary because it rightly stresses the objectivity of the Work of Christ, and it emphasises the holiness of God. The priest in the Old Testament also offered animal sacrifices to God as the representative of the people and these sacrifices speak of the real atonement of Christ which was to come. The destruction of the body of the animal speaks of the destruction of the sin. What was anticipated by the death of the animal now takes place in Christ. But here, the Priest not only offers a sacrifice, he is the sacrifice. He offers himself, his own body (Hebrews 9:12, 10:5, 10). There is an intimate connection between his priesthood, his sacrifice, and his humanity. Christ in some way genuinely "bore our sins in his own body on the tree" (1 Peter 2:14). Christ deals with the problem of our estrangement from

God at the radical depth of sin and guilt. As we saw above, sin is not external to humanity and to human beings (like a "thing" inside which can be removed). It is our whole being that is affected, and sin cannot be dealt with unless the old humanity itself dies. Christ takes our humanity, bearing our sins in his own body in order that the old humanity might be crucified and in him be raised incorruptible (Romans 6: 5-11).

The critical point is that Christ has fully identified himself with us in his incarnation, baptism, temptation, and death. This *identification* enables *representation:* both God to us and us to God (First Adam—Second Adam imagery, particularly in Romans 5:12-19). This is the core meaning of "vicarious;" Christ is our representative, taking our place. He does this "on behalf of us" or "for us," (the consistent Pauline usage) rather than "instead of us" (the Reformed position). The New Testament does not teach an absolute, exact substitution; rather, it seeks to make the point that all we lost in Adam is fully restored in Christ, who is the *Perfect Priest and Perfect Sacrifice.* In the Old Testament sacrificial system the identification and representation are explicit; the "laying on of hands" in Leviticus 1—7 is identification and representation not the transference of guilt (see also Isaiah 52:13—53:12). Furthermore, as our Priest, Christ ever lives to make intercession for us based on the *finished* work at the cross. We all need this work to atone for the inadvertent omissions, short-comings, mistakes, and defects that remain part of our humanity till the day of resurrection (Defects are all involuntary transgressions—see 1 John 2:1-2). We must now personally identify with Christ and accept his representative work on our behalf through personal faith, enabling his atoning work to become effective for us (baptism is "identification" in his death and resurrection).

3. The Kingly Work of Christ (Deity)

The work of Christ the King is foreshadowed in the life of King David; through his line one would arise who would defeat all the enemies of God's people. In the early Church, this motif was expressed through the *Christus Victor* model. By his death on the cross, Christ would defeat the enemy and bring deliverance from God's judgment. Through Christ, the powers of evil have been decisively defeated and the future promised reign of God has broken into the present and established the victory over sin, death, and hell. We live with the tension of the "already—not yet;" Christ has *already* won the victory, but it is *not yet* fully consummated— this awaits the Second Coming of Christ.

The Way of Salvation

In Western Christianity, soteriology (the doctrine of salvation) is generally formulated in two sharply differing positions: Augustinian and Pelagian. In Augustinianism humans were created holy, fell through pride, are now in bondage to sin, and cannot choose God. We need an infusion of grace to liberate the will from sinful bondage; this is irresistible and bestowed only on those whom God directly chooses (the elect). Salvation is therefore monergistic (wholly and solely the work of God). In Pelagianism, humans are created holy, but the fall does not result in the depravity of the whole race. The power to choose God remains. In this, we are assisted by grace, but it is not essential. Salvation is therefore synergistic (the work of both God and humans). In Wesleyanism, humans are created holy, and the fall results in human depravity with the will enslaved and unable to choose God. However, all people are recipients of prevenient grace through Christ and this "counteracts" depravity, enabling a free choice to be made. As such we may resist, or we may cooperate with it—to personally reject or accept Christ. We cannot choose God simply by ourselves, but through grace we are responsible before God for our choices (tension of inbeing sin—prevenient grace). Wesleyanism, then, avoids both Augustinianism and Pelagianism, though it easily reverts to either if the nuance is lost. For Wesley, no humans, strictly speaking, are merely in "a state of nature," for all have received prevenient grace. Sin comes not because we do not have grace but because we do not use the grace we have. For Wesley, salvation is *all* of grace; salvation is for *all;* not *all* are saved. In his understanding, salvation begins with *preventing grace.* This is the work of the Spirit that begins our deliverance, with our first understanding of God's will and of our violations of it; there is some tendency toward life, some degree of salvation. It is carried forward by *convincing grace* (repentance); it brings a larger measure of self-knowledge and further deliverance. We then experience proper *Christian salvation;* through grace we are saved by faith and it consists of *justification* and *sanctification.*[15]

The Doctrine of Free Grace

The interaction between sin and grace is the key to Wesley's doctrine of salvation, whereby the pessimism of the doctrine of original sin is overcome by the optimism of the doctrine of grace. Salvation is entirely the work of God. We do not contribute anything to it, for it is by grace alone (*sola gratia*) and is brought to the human race by the death of Christ. It stays the sentence of death for Adam, promising resurrection to him and his posterity; it cancels the guilt of original sin, and it reaches to every member of the human race. This grace is "free in all" and "free for all."

• "free for all"—Wesley's answer to Calvinism

• "free in all"—Wesley's affirmation that all the "good" we do is of grace; there is never any "merit in us"

Every person receives this gift of grace as an initial gift; it is irresistible. We cannot choose not to have it. Although, we may struggle with it, stifle it, or follow it to the presence of Christ. It restores a measure of freedom lacking in the bondage of inbeing sin, and it has performed its ultimate function when it brings us to Christ for justification. Wesley believed that God works; therefore, we *can* work. Secondly, God works; therefore, we *must* work. We do not sin because we do not have grace, rather, we sin because we do not use the grace we have. Since God first works in us, we are now able to respond to the offer of salvation, and a positive response enables us to receive more grace. If we refuse the grace offered, then we lose the grace we have already received. Wesley quotes Augustine: "He that made us without ourselves, will not save us without ourselves."[16] The bestowal of grace is always in God's hands. The "what" and the "when" are never ours to command, and easy assurances about the simplicity of the road to salvation are alien to Wesley.

Predestination and Election

Predestination/election is a point of major disagreement with our Reformed brothers and sisters, and Wesley's key works on the matter are *Predestination Calmly Considered* and *Thoughts upon Necessity*.[17] In Reformed (Calvinist) thought, all are not created for the same end; some are foreordained to eternal life (the elect) and others to eternal damnation (the reprobate). The choice of the elect and the reprobate is God's alone, and individuals can do nothing to merit or deny either choice. It is by God's eternal decrees that people are in one group or the other, and he is sovereign, that is to say, free to do whatever he wills (e.g. Parable of the Workers in the Vineyard, Matthew 20:13-15; Potter and the Clay, Romans 9:20-21). It is often summarised by the anacronym, T.U.L.I.P.—*T*otal depravity, *U*nconditional election, *L*imited atonement, *I*rresistible grace, *P*erseverance of the saints.

Wesley strongly affirmed:

- The Scriptures that declare God's willingness that all should be saved (John 3:16; Romans 5:18; 10:12; 2 Corinthians 5:15; 1 Timothy 2:3, 4; 4:10; 2 Peter 3:9; 1 John 4:14; Revelation 22:17).

- The Scriptures that declare that Christ came to save all, that he died for all, and that he atoned for all, even for those that finally perish (1 Corinthians 8:11; 1 Timothy 2:6; Hebrews 2:9; 1 John 2:1-2).

- The Scriptures that declare the justice of God (Ezekiel 18:2-31).

He rejected the argument that since all have sinned and deserve damnation, God may justly reprobate those he chooses not to save. This view of divine justice separates it from God's other attributes—mercy in particular. Romans 9 does not teach Calvinist predestination, but shows God's stated purpose in saving all who believe and damning all who do not believe. The sovereignty of God must never be separated from his other attributes (particularly his love). If the reprobate have no enabling power from God, God cannot justly condemn them for not doing what they never had the power to do. If grace is irresistible or not given, then neither group can do anything else but act as they do and are thus not responsible. In Wesley's opinion, the doctrine contradicts the sincerity of God in his offers of salvation to "whosoever," and undermines preaching the gospel. Above all, it contradicts the scriptural account of God's love and goodness for it is in the offer of salvation to every person that his glory is truly seen. In Wesleyan theology, election is the appointment of some people to do certain work in the world; it is an election for service and it does not have anything to do with salvation.

Repentance and Faith

Wesley agreed with the Reformers on justification but differed from them in insisting on the necessity of repentance (and works worthy of repentance, where there is opportunity) prior to justification. In Reformed thought, salvation is without qualification (monergistic); because of this infusion of grace, we believe and then begin to repent. Repentance is a life-long turning to God and it is the human side of the process of sanctification (which is God's work). This means that no good works can be done prior to justification. Wesley agreed that justification was entirely God's work but, because of prevenient grace, repentance and fruits meet, for repentance may go before justification if there is opportunity (Mark 1:15; Matthew 3:8). In repentance, the Holy Spirit uses the law as a means of awakening the soul "dead in trespasses and sins," bringing the conviction of being alienated from God and a rebel. Godly sorrow produced by the law mingled with the gospel "works repentance:" a conviction of sin, producing real desires and sincere resolutions of amendment. Through grace, the "fruits" are forgiving others, ceasing from evil, doing good, and in general, obeying God according to the measure of grace received. Since it is the law that the Spirit generally uses, Wesley terms this "legal" repentance. This becomes "evangelical" repentance as the convicted sinner begins to turn from sin to God himself. This led Wesley to repudiate the Reformed position that works done prior to justification were an abomination to God. Because they are performed by prevenient grace, they are good works. While repentance and its fruits cannot be neglected willingly, it is faith alone which justifies. Repentance and its fruits are only remotely necessary to faith, but faith is immediately and directly necessary to justification[18]—an example is the thief on the cross. Every Christian till we come to glory, "works *for* as well as *from* life."

Wesley rejected the idea that we are to do nothing before we come to faith in Christ; yet, our grace-enabled works have no part in meriting or purchasing our salvation from first to last, either in whole or in part.

Saving Faith

For Wesley, faith is defined as a sure trust and confidence in Christ bringing a sense of forgiveness. Our readiness for justification is not measured by our repentance but by our readiness to allow Christ's work within us. It requires an awareness that we are saved by faith alone. It is a gift of God alone—given not to those who are worthy but to the ungodly whose only plea is "God be merciful to me a sinner." Faith is primarily personal trust based on personal knowledge (a sure trust and confidence in God in Christ and a full reliance on the merits of Christ's death) and not mere intellectual assent to information.

Justification by Faith

Up to this point we have the preparatory work of the Spirit: preventing grace, convincing grace, evangelical repentance, and saving faith. "Proper Christian salvation" includes both justification and sanctification. Wesley wanted to make it plain that we are pardoned (justified) in order to participate (adoption). Wesley comes within "a hair's breadth of Calvinism" in opposing the Roman Catholic doctrine that good works are meritorious. For Wesley, as for Luther, our hope is not our own intrinsic righteousness, but that "alien righteousness" which comes through Christ. Unlike Luther's emphasis on forgiveness (and his weak conception of sanctification), Wesley is far more insistent upon the work of sanctification that begins at the moment of justification and which he believes embraces a subsequent moment in which the heart is cleansed from inbeing sin and perfected in love.

Justification is what God does *for* us through Christ. It is the objective frame of reference for our Christian existence; we always stand before

God accepted in Christ (Ephesians 1:6). By it we are saved from the guilt of sin and restored to the favour of God, all because of Christ's atoning sacrifice (Romans 3:21-31). The *act* of justification occurs at the moment we savingly trust Christ. The *present* justification we enjoy is ours as we permit our faith to work in love and as we walk in the light of God. *Final* justification is our future hope of acquittal on the day of judgement. Justification is to be seen primarily as God's "pardoning love" flowing from the sacrifice of Christ. God clearly justifies the ungodly on the basis of the work of Christ; yet, we cannot continue in sin as if God will always continue to pardon. The positive meaning of justification is "to be received into God's favour." God no longer imputes sin to our condemnation because of the work of Christ. Pardon and acceptance can be distinguished theologically but can never be divided experientially; at the moment of forgiveness, we are restored to the gracious position of a child of God. Two correlative terms for justification are *reconciliation* and *adoption*. Viewed from the standpoint of the renewal of broken fellowship, acceptance with God can be called reconciliation; the enmity has been changed by Christ's work to friendship and fellowship. Due to the work of Christ, enmity on God's part has been fully removed, and the only remaining obstacle is our enmity (see Romans 5:9-11). Viewed from the standpoint of the renewal of our true relation to God as Father, justification means adoption; this is closely tied to the witness of the Spirit.[19]

Wesley agrees that experientially one cannot distinguish between justification and new birth. It is certain that whoever is justified is also born of God, and whoever is born of God is also justified; although, theologically they are distinguished:

- Justification implies a relative change; the new birth implies a real change.

- God in justifying us does something *for* us; in the new birth, he does something *in* us.

- The former changes our outward relation to God so that we change from being enemies to being children; by the latter our inner being is changed so we move from being sinners to saints.

- The former restores us to divine favour; the latter begins restoring the image of God.

- The former takes away our guilt; the latter takes away the power of sin.[20]

Justification does not actually make us just and righteous; it only declares us to be such. It is the work of sanctification to bring about the real change. Sanctification is the immediate fruit of justification, and once more, cannot be distinguished experientially. Justification is what God does for us through his Son; sanctification is what God works in us by his Spirit. In the instant that we are born again there is a real as well as a relative change; we are then inwardly renewed by the power of God. From the moment of being born again, the gradual work of sanctification takes place as we are enabled by the Spirit to cease from sin and become more and more alive to God. In this relationship, we may earnestly seek entire sanctification, which is "love excluding sin, love filling the heart, taking up the whole capacity of the soul."[21]

Regeneration (The New Birth)

The necessity of the new birth arises from the fact that because of the Fall we are spiritually dead and our entire nature corrupt; being "born in sin" we must be "born again" (the new birth). The two doctrines of Justification and the New Birth are "fundamental" to Christianity; the former relates to the work God does *for us* (forgiving our sins), and the latter to the work God does *in us* (renewing our fallen nature, the beginning of sanctification).

- The new birth is instantaneous; sanctification is progressive.

- The new birth is the entrance to sanctification; the moment we are born again, our sanctification, our inward and outward holiness begins.

- In justification righteousness is imputed; at the new birth, it is imparted.

For Wesley, this means that "even babes in Christ were so far perfect as not to sin,"[22] when this is defined as an actual voluntary transgression of the law. To commit outward sin, we must progress from grace to sin by disregarding the checks of the Holy Spirit. So long as a believer remains in grace they do not commit actual sin. But by failing to mind the checks of the Spirit, a believer *may* sin. In every justified person there are two contrary principles, nature and grace ("flesh" and "Spirit" in Paul). While by grace the believer is saved from *actual* sin (or outward sin), they are very much aware, until entirely sanctified, of remaining *inward* sin. The *reign* of sin is broken, yet sin remains as an inward corruption of the affections. The guilt of sin is one thing, the power another, and the being yet another; believers are immediately delivered from the first two but not the third. Wesley was adamant that Christ cannot reign where sin reigns; neither will he dwell where sin is allowed, but he is and dwells in the heart of every believer who is fighting against all sin. Sin here is "inward sin," that is to say any sinful temper, passion, or affection in any kind or degree.

While we have the witness of the Spirit that we are truly children of God, we are aware that our will is not wholly resigned to the will of God. By "the repentance of believers," Wesley means the conviction, wrought by the Spirit, of this *remaining* sin in our hearts. It is identified as a tendency to self-will, idolatry, unbelief; as a spirit, a perversion of our self-life; as a bent to sinning, with a bias toward self and away from God.[23] Though we become very much aware of remaining inward sin, we must not throw away our confidence in God, nor must we rest in the awareness of such sin, but seek to open our life more and more to Christ. In this way, we discover that further grace will purify the heart and perfect us in love. Sin is ended by the gift of an unbroken relationship with Christ. It is both a crisis and a process as we open our lives to the light of Christ's presence and continue to walk by faith in that light. Wesley was deeply convinced that there was no easy cure for inbeing sin; it is not enough to simply "preach the gospel and apply the promises," for to oversimplify the problem is to make matters worse. Consequently, as primary and indispensable as preaching the gospel is, it must be accompanied by nurturing discipleship. This underscores the key role of the "means of grace" and for close pastoral oversight to identify the causes and apply the remedies. Wesley believed that the usual cause of the "wilderness state" so common among Christians is the slighting of the means of grace, and the remedy will be found in participating in them (See Chapter 9, "The Church"). So, the repentance of believers is the conviction of sin remaining in our hearts (it remains but does not reign). It is the conviction of sin still cleaving to our words and actions, and we find this to be true when we least expect it—the taint of pride or self-will, of unbelief or idolatry. It is the conviction of helplessness because holy living is of grace from first to last. If we fail to acknowledge this remaining sin and repent of it, we lock ourselves out from being "perfected in love."

QUESTIONS FOR REFLECTION

1. How would you explain "atonement" to a new Christian?

2. In what ways do Wesleyans agree with the Augustinian position on salvation and where do we differ?

3. How can grace enable us to have a "free" response to God's offer of salvation without compelling it?

4. What is the difference between a Reformed and a Wesleyan understanding of the relationship between repentance and faith? What practical difference does it make in our witness?

5. Can you explain the difference between justification and sanctification?

6. Can a new Christian live a life, by God's grace, that is victorious over sin?

CHAPTER 6

THE DOCTRINE OF ENTIRE SANCTIFICATION

WE BELIEVE

That believers are to be sanctified wholly, subsequent to regeneration, through faith in the Lord Jesus Christ

Entire Sanctification is a core, doctrinal emphasis in Methodism in general and in the Church of the Nazarene specifically. It is one of the main reasons for our existence as a denomination. It is also the most misunderstood of our doctrines. Therefore, a fuller development is offered in the book *Embracing a Doctrine of Holiness,* which is another volume in this *Frameworks for Lay Leadership* series. Here, we will give a brief synopsis of this important doctrine.

At the heart of John Wesley's theological understanding was the claim that the essential nature of God is love, and this is expressed relationally within the Triune Godhead and then with the creatures that God made. That means we are created to be "persons-in-community," and it requires a consistency and integration of life lived for God in every relationship—a "wholeness" of life. This is where the biblical concern for holiness is seen—not as some abstract quality or standard, but with reference to the quality of the divine love that shaped us in creation and is shared with us as an intrinsic element of our human nature. To love as

God loves is to be holy as God is holy because divine love and selfishness are absolutely incompatible. To love the Lord is to be formed by that bond, and this is where ethics, morality, obedience, and duty fit; they all flow from a right relationship.

The Nature of Entire Sanctification

The "Great Commandment" is simply to love God and then neighbour with our whole being. Entire sanctification is not primarily about separation from that which is sinful but a positive engagement with God and the neighbour from a heart of pure love. Love is, therefore, at the heart of Wesley's understanding of sanctification:

> Love is the sum of Christian sanctification: it is the one kind of holiness which is found, only in various degrees, in the believers who are distinguished by St. John into 'little children, young men, and fathers'. The difference between one and the other properly lies in the degree of love."[24]

This theological framework affirms that the goal of salvation in Christ is to "'love the Lord they God with all thy soul, and thy neighbour as thyself'. The Bible declares, 'Love is the fulfilling of the Law,' 'the end of the commandment,' of all the commandments which are contained in the oracles of God."[25] This fullness of love Wesley terms "Christian Perfection" and it is defined in terms of our present human condition, not our condition before the fall or after the resurrection. Loving relationships in this context are inherently transformational; you cannot remain the same if you are in genuine, loving connection with another because of an authentic desire to please them through shared conversations and interests. Loving another with integrity means you cannot do, say, or think things that would damage or diminish the other and still claim to truly love. Wesley contended that much of the rejection of the doctrine was due to misunderstanding its nature, equating it with a "sinless perfection."

We willingly allow, and continually declare, there is no such perfection in this life as implies either a dispensation from doing good and attending all the ordinances of God; or a freedom from ignorance, mistake, temptation, and a thousand infirmities necessarily connected with flesh and blood.[26]

By defining entire sanctification in terms of loving God and neighbour in this present body and conditions, Wesley was confident that the one who "experiences this is scripturally perfect."[27] Entire sanctification was the initial experience of the fullness of the love of God and neighbour, and Christian perfection encompassed both the initial moment and the ever-deepening continuance of that relationship. Wesley admonished his people: "let *love* not visit you as a transient guest, but be the constant ruling temper of your soul."[28]

The greatest challenge to Wesley's understanding of Christian perfection came from those in the Reformed theological tradition, who denied that it was possible for any human being to perfectly conform to God's law in every particular. This was a point that troubled many within Methodism itself, and it was of critical importance to clearly distinguish between sin (for which Wesley believed the Christian was culpable) and infirmities (for which he believed the Christian was not culpable). Wesley agreed with his critics that Adam as created was perfectly capable of meeting all of God's requirements since he had no defect in his body, understanding, or affections. Wesley argued that since fallen humanity could not possibly conform to every requirement of the initial covenant, God had now established a covenant of grace, and all the requirements of the law were met fully in Christ; so that, the one who believed in him would be fully accepted by God. Living in a corrupted body did mean that "mistakes" would arise, not from a defect of love, but a defect of knowledge. As long as there was "no concurrence of the will," there was no sin. He was positive that a relationship with God centred in love could be unbroken if the Christian acknowledged the mistake and its consequences as soon as they were aware of it and sought the continuing benefit of the atonement immediately.

Experiencing Entire Sanctification

The strength of Wesley's doctrine is in the awareness that the work of sanctification is a gift, a divine work wrought by God and to be accepted by faith. There is a gradual work of transformation prior to and after this "moment." But there is the promise of the immediate gift of a heart filled with God's love. Wesley admitted that God can work as he chooses, and he may bring people into this experience very quickly and without any perceptible gradual work at all. It is the expectation of the fulfilment of the promises of Christ in our life that is critical; the faith that leads to entire sanctification is essentially a conviction that what God has promised he is able to perform and that he is able and willing to do it *now*. Just as we are justified by faith, so we are sanctified wholly by faith. This makes faith the condition, and the only condition, of sanctification, exactly as it is of justification. Christians need to come to the place of believing that God can save them from all remaining sin in their heart. This is based on his promises in such Scriptures as Deuteronomy 30:6; Ezekiel 36:25, 27, 29; Psalm 130:8; Luke 1:68-69, 72-75; and 2 Corinthians 7:1. Wesley said that if a person did not expect an instantaneous change, then it was unlikely that they would ever experience Christian perfection before death.

Maintaining a Life of Pure Love

Wesley believed that this experience of Christian perfection could be lost, as testimony, observation, and the Scriptures confirmed (see especially Hebrews 10:29; 1 John 2:15; 1 Thessalonians 5:16; Ephesians 4:30). He said Christians must either go forward or backwards in their relationship with God; we cannot stand still. Spiritual growth may be swift and noticeable or it may be more like the slow, imperceptible growth of a tree. This makes it all the more important to understand that our ability to think, evaluate, and judge is compromised by our current bodily existence. It is from our wrong judgments that wrong words and actions flow, as well as wrong affections. Wesley called these "infirmities" and they had to be clearly distinguished from sin. For the latter, we were clearly culpable and under condemnation; for the former, there was no culpability and therefore no condemnation. To "set the state of perfection too high is the surest way to drive it out of the world,"[29] and to imply that perfection in love requires a total freedom from mistakes or human infirmities is to set it too high.

Distinguishing between sin and infirmities is a major pastoral problem, and a static theological distinction often proves to be inadequate in actual lived experience. The only certain help is to be found in the ministry of the Spirit, both personally and communally, to discern our true intention. The closer we come to Christ the more aware we are of the reality of these "infirmities" and the deeper the longing to be rid of them. We will always need the work of Christ as our faithful High Priest because we are always in danger of classifying proper sins as innocent mistakes and excusing them or minimising and excusing failures without seeking their correction. Here we see the key importance of developing a deeper self-understanding that no longer seeks to hide ourselves from ourselves, refusing to admit our shortcomings or revelling in our defects ("That's just the way I am"). The Spirit can now show us the truth without us fighting him. There is clearly an "already—not yet" tension in Wesley's understanding of Christ's work. We *already* experience a great deliverance from the power of sin, but it is *not yet* a final deliverance in which all things will be made new.

QUESTIONS FOR REFLECTION

1. Why is the doctrine of entire sanctification such a source of disagreement between Wesleyan and Reformed churches?

2. How would you explain our understanding of Christian perfection to your Reformed friend? In your opinion, what point would produce the biggest disagreement?

3. How would you explain our understanding of Christian perfection to a new believer in your church? Consider writing out this doctrine in your own language. This will help assure that you understand it well and are able to communicate simply to others.

4. What do you understand by the term "infirmity" and how it relates to "sin" in Wesleyan theology? Why is this distinction so important to our understanding of entire sanctification?

CHAPTER 7

THE DOCTRINE OF ASSURANCE

WE BELIEVE
The Holy Spirit bears witness to the new birth, and also to the entire sanctification of believers

The words of Wesley reflecting on his experience at a meeting at Aldersgate Street in London on 24 May 1738 are significant: "I felt I did trust in Christ, Christ alone, for salvation; and an assurance was given me that He had taken away *my* sins, even *mine,* and saved *me* from the law of sin and death."[30]. This witness of the Spirit was drawn from the key scripture of Romans 8:16 and is an "inward impression on the soul" that testifies to us that we are now God's child. This "inward impression" may bring about feelings, but the "impression" is self-authenticating and cannot be clearly described to those who have not received it. This is then confirmed by the witness of our own spirit through such evidences as repentance, a consciousness of passing from "death to life," an awareness of transformation, the fruit of the Spirit, a glad obedience to the commands of God, and a "good conscience" towards God. While it is easy to mistake our feelings for true assurance, these scriptural tests can be applied to see whether the claim is genuine (the "fruit of the Spirit"). In all of this we must never presume to rest in any supposed testimony of the Spirit, which is separate from the fruit of the Spirit. Wesley believed that the witness of the Spirit was the privilege of all the children of God; however, it is not *essential* to justification.

For Wesley, the witness covers the whole ground of Christian experience, both justification and sanctification. In the New Testament, the references to the witness of the Spirit in Romans and Galatians are to adoption not to entire sanctification. His conviction on this issue arises from the general tenor of Scripture and the "experience" of many Christians. He was convinced that it was the common privilege of every Christian to experience the witness of the Holy Spirit to the reality of entire sanctification, just as it was to their new birth. Wesley warned his followers not to trust in their feelings but to base their confidence in God's Word; otherwise their trust would be in the feelings and not in Christ. Likewise, negative feelings were not in themselves an evidence of sin. He wrote that "a will steadily and uniformly devoted to God is essential to a state of sanctification, but not an uniformity of joy or peace or happy communion with God."[31] These can rise and fall in degrees and are affected by the body or Satan. It is important to note that an experience of assurance is not a guarantee of final salvation. Life in Christ is a relationship of love and this can either flourish or deteriorate. If we continue to refuse the love of God, then we will walk away from the relationship and if we persist in that, our salvation is lost.

QUESTIONS FOR REFLECTION

1. Practically, how important is the doctrine of assurance in the life of a Christian?

2. How would you counsel a Christian worried about their lack of "feeling" loved by Christ?

CHAPTER 8

THE DOCTRINE OF LAST THINGS

WE BELIEVE
Our Lord will return, the dead will be raised, and the final judgment will take place

Eschatology is the study of "last things" and deals with all the events surrounding the return of Christ in which the old order will pass away and the new order will be fully perfected. We presently live in the tension between what Christ has *already* accomplished and what has *not yet* taken place. The key focus in all this is the person of Jesus Christ, the Last One (Mark 1:15; Revelation 22:13; John 13:31; Hebrews 1:2; 2 Timothy 1:10) and on being his disciples here and now. The call is to be "faithful in the meantime." The Last Days began with the Christ-Pentecost Event (Acts 2:17; Hebrews 1:2) and the future age of the Spirit is already invading the present evil age (Romans 12:2; Galatians 1:4; 2 Timothy 1:10; Hebrews 6:5). Christians live in the tension of the fact they have already received their resurrection life, yet await bodily resurrection beyond death (John 3:16, 36; 11:25-26; Ephesians 2:6). We need to be aware of the danger of "wanting to know too much" because the biblical language about the future is primarily symbolic. We gain the best insight into God's actions in the future by looking at what he has already done.

A Wesleyan Perspective on Eschatology and the Difference It Makes

Eschatological beliefs have a profound impact on our actions within this present world: are we looking for an escape to heaven or are we seeking to be agents of transformation while awaiting the renewal of all things? Eschatology embodies our convictions about the "how" and the "when" of God's victory over all the powers of evil will come. Overly confident prophecies are nothing new. Jesus warned his disciples that "false prophets" would misinterpret the signs of the times, deceive, and alarm believers (Matthew 24:4-25). He urged his followers to be properly sceptical: "If anyone tells you [they know how to interpret the signs of the end], do not believe it!" (Matthew 24:26-27). Sadly, too many Christians have ignored Jesus's warning.

The official position of the Church of the Nazarene on the subject of the Second Coming of Jesus Christ stands fully within the historic mainstream of Christian thought. All the classic, ecumenical Christian creeds have been brief and concise on this subject. The brief statement in the *Manual* adequately summarizes all we can say with confidence about eschatology based on the Apostles' Creed and the Nicene Creed. For Nazarenes, our brief statement is the result of studied silence, not a license to speculate freely. Unfortunately, those who have written and preached most extensively on the subject of eschatology have generally been advocates of bizarre views. Wesleyan views are more adequate because they are more dependent on ancient Christian tradition, not innovations introduced only during the 19th century. The difference is seen historically in three models of millennialism. The millennium is a time of *shalom* (peace), justice, and flourishing on this earth (see Isaiah) before the recreation of all things (see Daniel). For centuries Revelation 20 has been the most disputed chapter in this most symbolic book of the Bible. Little of what is popularly assumed about the so-called "Millennial Reign of Christ" is actually found in Revelation 20, yet this is the only biblical passage that explicitly mentions it. John's obvious motive in presenting this vision is not information but inspiration—to encourage the Christians of Asia to remain faithful until death. We certainly misinterpret the book if we fail to accept the same encouragement. Each of the verses of Revelation 20:4-6 mentions the Millennium—the thousand years. The context of these verses between Revelation 20:2-3 and 7 leads to the conclusion that the period of Satan's confinement and the reign of Christ coincide. The controversy centres around the meaning of the thousand-year reign of Christ reported in Revelation 20:4-6.

There are four major schools of interpretation of the Millennium and equally devout Christians have upheld the first three views since the earliest centuries of the church.

1. *Premillennialism:* Christ must return before we can have true peace and justice; he will establish an earthly kingdom of 1,000 years before the eternal order begins. This is arguably the common view in the earliest church, when Christianity was a minority and persecuted faith. Essentially, it is pessimistic about the difference the church can make in world.

2. *Amillennialism:* There is no need for a future time of peace and justice on this earth because the church age already expresses God's rule here. This was common soon after Christianity became the established religion of the Roman Empire in the 4th century.

3. *Postmillennialism:* Christ will return only after the church (through the Spirit) has spread the gospel throughout the world and ushered in a time of peace and justice. This was the dominant view of Euro-American Protestants, 1750–1920 and was optimistic about the impact of evangelism and social reform on the world.

Both Postmillennialism and Amillennialism understand the number 1,000 in a figurative sense. You can find examples of historic premillennialism, postmillennialism, and amillennialism in Wesleyan churches. It is the impact of the horrors of World War I and the Great Depression that saw a fourth view creep into Wesleyan circles.

4. *Dispensationalism:* This appears for the first time in the 1830s and was popularised by Edward Irving. It introduced the notion of the "Rapture," where the saints alive at the time of the great tribulation will be caught up secretly to heaven. This was adopted and

popularised by J. N. Darby, and introduced to the wider western evangelical church through the notes in C. I. Scofield's Reference Bible and the preaching of evangelist Dwight L. Moody. In more recent days it has been promoted by the likes of Hal Lindsey, Jerry Falwell, Pat Robertson, Timothy and Beverley LaHaye.

Dispensationalism is a distinctive kind of premillennialism with several novel views. Perhaps its most controversial innovation, which distinguishes it from all three classical millennial theories, is the separation of the Second Coming into a two-part event—a secret Rapture that is to precede the public revelation by as many as seven years. This doctrine of a secret Rapture belongs exclusively to dispensational premillennialism. The only biblical passage that comes close to mentioning the term "rapture" is 1 Thessalonians 4:16-17. There the "catching up" of living believers is not pictured as an event distinguishable from the Second Coming of Christ. The imagery is clearly tied to the realities of living in the Roman Empire where trumpets announce the arrival of an important dignitary. The people go out to meet the person as they are arriving, and then they return together into the city. It is a symbolic picture of the true King (Christ) coming "down" to permanently dwell with his people in the New Jerusalem. He is met by his people (the "up") and then escorted back into the city (the "down") to dwell with them eternally.

The Second Coming

The term Second Coming refers to the promised return of the crucified and risen Jesus (John 14:2-3; Acts 1:10-11) to consummate what was begun with his first Advent. The timing rests with God and is unknown to us (Mark 13:32-33). His return will be visible, sudden, cosmic, and glorious (Revelation 1:7; Matthew 24:27, 43; 1 Thessalonians 5:2; 2 Peter 3:10; Philippians 2:10-11). It is clearly to be anticipated by all faithful Christians and not feared.

General Resurrection

The doctrine of resurrection affirms the goodness of the physical world God created. The historic belief of the Church is in the "resurrection of the body" (this is the language used in all the creeds) and not the "immortality of the soul" (1 Corinthians 15:44). Only God is essentially immortal (1 Timothy 6:16), but we are "clothed" with it as a gift of grace (1 Corinthians 15:53-54). Biblically and historically, the "soul" is the "life principle" of a unified person and not a separate part of their existence. In the resurrection, we are given a "spiritual body" that is still physical and is the perfect expression of life in Christ. There is a tension in the biblical account between, on the one hand, 2 Corinthians 5:1-7 and Philippians 1:21-24 (full participation in Christ and life with him on dying) and, on the other hand, 1 Corinthians 15:23 and Philippians 3:20-21 (resurrection at the last day). Philippians contains both "images." Therefore, Paul is clearly not troubled by the apparent contradiction. Over against this we have the simple affirmation of 1 Thessalonians 4:13-15 and 2 Corinthians 5:3-10. The link is always with Jesus's resurrection; he is the first one, but will not be the only one, to be resurrected (John 5:25-26; Romans 6:5; 1 Corinthians 15:16, 20-23; 1 Peter 1:3-4). This event will occur at Jesus's return (1 Corinthians 15:16, 20-23). All will participate in the one and only resurrection (Acts 24:15; Romans 14:10; John 5:28-29; Revelation 20:11-15; Matthew 16:27; Romans 2:15-16; 2 Timothy 4:12). The Bible gives us little detail, but we know that every Christian will be like Christ (1 John 3:20; Philippians 3:21). The final vision includes a transformed creation (Revelation 21:1). In the meantime, we are confident that death cannot separate us from God and his love (Romans 8:38-39; 1 Corinthians 15:53; Psalm 23).

Judgement

God as holy love means that coercion cannot be at the heart of a personal relationship with God. There are real consequences for our choices, and to reject condemnation as one possible outcome is to deny the reality of our freedom. The basis of divine judgement is our response to the love of God revealed to us in Christ (2 Corinthians 5:10; Matthew 12:36; 25:1-46). It is a judgement that has already started (John 3:18; Romans 1:18-32) but will be finally pronounced after death (Revelation 20:11-15). Biblically, judgement is not primarily condemnation; rather, it is to establish the right order of things (Luke 1:46-55). It may take place immediately upon death (2 Corinthians 5:10; Hebrews 9:27) or at a "final assize" (Revelation 20:11-15). The Bible makes it plain (Matthew 10:30; 20:16; 25:31-46; Hebrews 10:26-31) that God, who knows our hearts, will judge justly.

Hell: Place of Separation

The significance of human beings to God is accompanied by accountability (Daniel 12:2) for our attitude and actions toward the offer of salvation through Jesus Christ (Matthew 25:41-46; 2 Thessalonians 1:6-8) and not God's reluctance to save us (2 Peter 3:9; 1 Timothy 2:4). It is Jesus himself who often spoke of "hell" (Mark 9:43, 45, 47; Matthew 5:22; 8:12; 13:42; 25:30, 46); and he makes it plain that it was never intended for human occupation but for Satan and his accomplices (Matthew 25:41). At its heart, it is a place of final separation from God, his people, and his renewed creation (Matthew 12:32; Luke 18:30; 2 Thessalonians 1:9; Galatians 1:4; Colossians 1:26). Within a Wesleyan framework, we do not believe that God "sends" anyone to hell; it is the consequence of their own free choice to persistently refuse God's grace. It is the end of the road we have personally chosen to take. Traditionally, hell is eternal (Matthew 8:8; 25:41, 46; 2 Thessalonians 1:9). It must be admitted that the word can mean a long, indefinite period, but if we take this view then it must apply to "eternal life" as well. Eternal consequences for temporal offences is no more unreasonable than eternal life for temporal grace. Some theologians have rejected the notion of endless punishment and have proposed the annihilation of the unrighteous as the answer, based on such passages as Matthew 10:28; 2 Thessalonians 1:9; 2 Peter 3:7, 11-13; and Revelation 20:14. This view of "conditional immortality" is held by such people as John Stott, Philip Hughes, Clark Pinnock, and E. Stanley Jones, who do not find an eternal cosmic dualism acceptable. In their view, God only raises the just (or raises all for judgement before then annihilating the unjust). They believe fire and death indicate destruction and "eternal" signifies the result rather than the continuous act. Some have seen the eventual redemption of the whole race as the answer (Origen, Schleiermacher, Barth). However, *universalism* has not been an orthodox belief. Perhaps C. S. Lewis said it best when he wrote that the door to hell is locked from the inside, and it is the outcome of a totally self-centred life.[32]

Heaven: Place of Glory

Both the Old and New Testaments affirm that God has not rejected the world as such (its physicality), but "this world in its present form" (1 Corinthians 7:31). The promises of Isaiah 2:4 and 65:17-25 indicate a return to "Eden" described as a perfectly good and perfectly natural new heaven and new earth. This is strongly affirmed in Romans 8:19-24, with a renewed creation (especially focused on the earth) as a suitable environment for resurrected saints. In Revelation 21 the New Jerusalem "descends" from the heavens to earth and provides a totally new environment for the saints with God's very presence among them (see Revelation 22:1-5). It will be a bodily experience, and it will not involve the loss of our human individuality. Although the nature of the "body" and heavenly "physicality" is beyond us to know at this point, Jesus's resurrection body may give some clues. Nevertheless, we know that it will be a glorious community living in the fullness of love and participating without hindrance in the life of the Trinity. It does seem to be a place of varied rewards and tasks—see the parables and 1 Corinthians 3:10-15; it will be filled with challenges and achievements, all within the riches of perfect love for God and each other.

QUESTIONS FOR REFLECTION

1. What are some of the dangers faced by Christians who focus their attention on trying to work out a date for Christ's return?

2. Why do you think the Church of the Nazarene has not required a more specific belief regarding the timing and events associated with Christ's return?

3. Why is it so important to hold a belief in the "resurrection of the body" rather than the "immortality of the soul"?

4. What is the relationship between love, freedom, consequences for choices, and the existence of both heaven and hell? Why is an understanding of this relationship so important?

CHAPTER 9

THE DOCTRINE OF THE CHURCH

WE BELIEVE
*In the Church, the community that confesses Jesus Christ as Lord,
the covenant people of God made new in Christ, the Body of
Christ called together by the Holy Spirit through the Word*

Each section of the Agreed Statement of Belief in the *Manual* of the Church of the Nazarene starts with "We believe…" This is the confession of a community and not just an isolated individual. This is made clear in Article XI of our Articles of Faith given above.

The Nature of the Church: A Wesleyan Perspective

Tom Noble reminds us that the Church is one of the few places where Christian theology can be observed. Indeed, for many it is their one and only contact with Christianity. Several people view the church as a building, a denomination, an institution, or an organisation. Unfortunately, the doctrine of the Church has not been a major emphasis of theology across the centuries. However, it is now becoming more of a focus due to the ecumenical movement, church growth, and missions. It involves a discussion concerning the place of the Church and its mission in a multicultural and multi-faith environment.

The Church of the Nazarene, as a Wesleyan church, has its roots in the Church of England, as well as in the Free Church (also called the Believer's Church) tradition. These two streams influence our denomination and its ecclesiology (understanding of the Church). From the Free Church tradition we inherit a focus on the individual and his or her personal decision to follow Christ. This results in holding to believer's baptism only and seeing the church as a voluntary collection of such individuals. This tradition arises from those who are reacting against formality in worship, valuing spontaneity in worship as the evidence of the presence of the Spirit. Our Anglican roots begin with a corporate view of the church and then moves to the personal. This is clearly more characteristic of the biblical viewpoint and still characterises many societies in the non-Western world. This tradition values the ancient liturgy of the church in which all participate, as well as the place of the sacraments as a frequent feature of the worship service. Holding these perspectives in a healthy tension is not an easy task.[33]

Biblical Definition of the Church

The Church is a community created by the Spirit through Christ to be both a worshipping and a missional community. Both of these movements are essential, just as life can only be sustained if we both breathe in and breathe out. The word "church" (Greek *ekklesia*) is only found in the Gospels in Matthew 16:18 and 18:17, but it is common in Acts and the epistles, especially in Paul. The Old Testament uses the Hebrew and Greek equivalent terms to refer to the covenant community of Israel. In the New Testament it can refer to local gatherings of believers (1 Corinthians 1:2; 2 Corinthians 1:1; Galatians 1:2; 1 Thessalonians 1:1), all believers in a given city (Acts 8:1; 13:1), and all believers in a broad area (Acts 9:31; 1 Corinthians 16:19). It is essentially a "household" gathering where the ministry of the Spirit is primarily communal and not individual and each local church is a manifestation in time and space of the total community. In other words, there is only one Church (Matthew 16:18; Ephesians 1:22-23; 3:10, 21; 4:4; 5:23, 24, 32; 1 Corinthians 10:32; 11:22; 12:28; Colossians 1:18, 24). As such, it comprises all believers—past, present, and future (Hebrews 12:23). The primary expression of the church is the visible, gathered, local congregation that meets regularly.

Biblical Images of the Church

There are several different biblical images used to speak about the Church:

- *The People of God* (2 Corinthians 6:16): This emphasises God's initiative in choosing and creating this people (2 Thessalonians 2:13-14; 1 Thessalonians 1:4; cf. Exodus 15:13, 16; Numbers 14:8; Deuteronomy 32:9-10; Isaiah 62:4; Jeremiah 12:7-10; Hosea 1:9-10; 2:23). It is an exclusive claim as we are called to be his covenant people without reservation and without divided loyalty. Both Israel and the Church are called into existence by God and elected for service. The continuity of Israel and the Church is theological, originating in Genesis 12:3 where "mission" is the crucial context.

- *The Bride:* This is clearly implied in 2 Corinthians 11:1f; Ephesians 5:27-32; Revelation 19:7-8. The Old Testament imagery focuses on "separation" to the new family and "separation" from parents; and so, the Church is separated to Christ and from the world. We are called to live worthy of our "betrothal," which is symbolised by our baptism.

- *The Body of Christ:* The analogy of the human and the Christian body is the most extended image. It is mentioned nineteen times and only in the Pauline epistles, making it Paul's most frequent metaphor. The church is the body, and Christ is the Head (Colossians 1:18; 2:9-10). This emphasises the Church as a single functional unit that works together for the health of the whole in a reciprocal relationship of interdependence and interrelationship. Paul never writes of the "body of Christians," only the "Body of Christ." Individualism leads to a dysfunctional body because "wholeness" is essential to "holiness." A divided body is a polluted body (see 1 Corinthians 12 where none can live without the other; and 1

Corinthians 11 where a rebuke is directed to a divided church at the Lord's Table). The Church is an extension of the Incarnation, but not in an absolute institutional way; there is a constant process of coming to completion with the continuity found in *Word* and *Sacrament*, not in the institution.

• *The Temple of the Holy Spirit* (1 Corinthians 3:16-17; 6:19; 12:13; Ephesians 2:21-22; 1 Peter 2:5): It is the Spirit who imparts life (Galatians 5:22-23), holiness and purity (1 Corinthians 6:19-20), brings power for service and mission (Acts 1:8; John 14:12), and imparts gifts and graces (1 Corinthians 12:11).

• *The Family of God:* This is possibly the dominant image in the New Testament, indicating a place to belong, to be secure. There are numerous references to God as Father, the Son, the children of God, the household, and Christians as brothers and sisters (Mark 10:28-30; Romans 16; Colossians 4:7; Philemon 7, 15-16; Philippians 2:22; 3:1). This image underpins the whole argument of Galatians and Romans (Galatians 3:28; Romans 3:21-26; 8:14-17; see also, 1 Peter 1—2; John 1:12; 13:34-35). It reminds us of the need to have realistic expectations and be patient with one another (Galatians 5:22; Colossians 3:13; Romans 15:7; 1 Peter 3:8-9; Romans 14) and to be there for one another (Acts 2:41-47; 4:32-37; 1 John 3:17-18; 1 Corinthians 16; 2 Corinthians 8).

The Marks of the Church

The Church is a sociocultural reality and it always takes on historically conditioned forms. Even in the Book of Acts, all its "forms" were borrowed from the surrounding Jewish and pagan environments. For Wesleyans, there is no point trying to regain the forms of worship, organisation, or practices found in a supposed "pure" New Testament church; the focus must be on the same presence of the Spirit in our current and developing forms. The four classical marks of the church (unity, holiness, catholicity, apostolicity) were first formally stated in the Creed of Constantinople (Nicene Creed) in AD 381. They were an experienced reality before a doctrinal statement.

- *Unity:* The focus of Jesus's high priestly prayer in John 17. The unity is found in Christ (Ephesians 4:5; Philippians 2:2-8) and all who are identified by faith with him are "in him" (Colossians 2:6-7, 10-11) and share in the unity of his person (John 15, Vine and branches; a bond of mutual self-giving love). The subjective ground of unity is the work of the Spirit, who is the Spirit of Christ. "Christ in me" and "Christ in you" cannot be at variance (see the "fellowship" of Acts; 2 Corinthians 13:14; Philippians 2:1; 1 Corinthians 1:9). Baptism is the ritual sign of Christian unity. For Wesley, the unity of the Church is based upon Christian fellowship in the Holy Spirit and not a formal institutional unity.

- *Holiness:* This is essential because we are the people of God, the body of Christ, and indwelt by the Spirit. Wesley commented that the holiness of the Church is fostered in the discipline of grace which guides and matures the Christian life from its threshold in justifying grace to its fullness in sanctifying grace.

- *Catholicity* (meaning universal): Both John 12:32 and Philippians 2:6-11 affirm that there is a universal scope to salvation with no divisive distinctions based on human differences of race, culture, language, social status, education, gender, or age (see Galatians 3:27-28). Christ is "for all," the Atonement is "for all" (Galatians 3:28), and "all" are invited to the banquet by Jesus. For Wesley, the catholicity of the Church is defined by the universal outreach of redemption and the one essential community of all true believers in Christ. This does not mean that we should not celebrate God's richness in gifting and gracing in a beautiful harmonic diversity—the biblical mark is unity and not uniformity (which is profoundly unscriptural).

- *Apostolicity:* This is grounded in God's mission to the world through Jesus Christ (Hebrews 1:1ff) and the gift of the Spirit to all believers as witnesses (Matthew 28:19-20; Acts 1:8; John 20:21). It involves both a message (Gospel) and a messenger. For Wesley, the apostolicity of the Church is gauged by the succession of apostolic doctrine in those who have been faithful to the apostolic witness.

The Means of Grace and the Sacraments

Wesley affirmed that by nature we are self-idolatrous and slaves to the things of this world, and it is only a life of discipline that can wean us from our worldly attachments and free us for God's service. We have the promise of God for deliverance from remaining sin, but we need to "wait" for it carefully. It is true, we receive this gift by simple faith, but God does not and will not give that faith unless we seek it with all diligence in the way he has ordained. The *means of grace* are the outward signs, words, or actions ordained of God and appointed to this end, to be the ordinary channels whereby he might convey to us preventing, justifying, or sanctifying grace.[34] There is no inherent power in them and they have value to us only when we see that God alone has power to pardon, sanctify, and grant us the gift of his Spirit. It is the God in whom we trust who has appointed these means as channels through which he normally grants us his gifts. Christ is the only source of grace, but he has appointed means whereby we may receive his grace.

Wesley was thoroughly Protestant and believed that only two sacraments (Holy Communion and Baptism) were "ordained" by God, plus a number of other "means" available through our worship and spiritual practices. Wesley's concern was for us to experience both the presence of God himself and the transforming power of his grace that shapes our character. It is grace alone that *empowers* our responsive reception without *compelling* that reception. The means of grace must enable and encourage the presence and growth of love through an ongoing relationship with God. They must not be substituted for the relationship or become an end in themselves. They provide practices which facilitate critical self-awareness, which is meant to increase self-knowledge of our hidden deceptions, mixed motives, and societal conditioning. They encourage accountable discipleship, self-examination, and repentance within a community of forgiveness and love. They assist in avoiding presumption by continually presenting the atoning and mediational work of Christ and the "not yet" aspect of the Kingdom which evokes repentance.

The key means of grace are such things as remaining in the Church, its liturgy, and sacraments. Corporate worship is not a matter of duty but of sustenance and to fail here is to miss spiritual nurture. Wesley wrote of the importance of both fellowship and discipline in community through small groups. He noted that no matter how great the initial conversion, if there were no regular societies, no discipline, no order, or connection, then the vast majority of the new Christians would fall away. Wesley sought the abandonment of our old way of life, which was rooted in the values of the world and subversive of faith, and a fostering of a Christian counter-culture that was to be salt and light *in* the world but not *of* the world. He emphasised the role of works of mercy that kept the Christian focused on service. This fostered growth, since in loving the world there is rarely mutuality, and mercy forms, deepens, and expresses the love of neighbour. "Rules" were always a means of grace and not ends in themselves; all is to be governed by the "rule of love" and no "rule of discipline" can be kept exactly without at some point undermining the law of love (e.g. "do no work on the Sabbath" may need to be overruled by the need to help another). Wesley emphasised the place of *corporate worship, prayer and fasting,* and *searching the Scriptures.* The Bible provides all that we need to form and shape our Christian life based on and in response to the character of God revealed in them; there is always a linking of prayer and Scripture.

The Sacraments

The word "sacrament" derives from a Latin word that was usually used to translate the New Testament Greek word *mysterion* (meaning "mystery"). A sacrament is commonly described as an outward and visible sign of an inward and spiritual grace. In the sacraments, we are reminded that God may accomplish spiritual ends through material means, which can be a carrier of divine grace. Grace is neither a thing nor a substance. However, it may be conveyed by way of things—bread, wine, water (just as a garden hose can "convey" the life-giving water). No amount of understanding, intellect, and reason can fully grasp all that is involved because there is always an element of mystery.

The Sacrament of Baptism (A Means of Justifying Grace)

In the New Testament, baptism is commanded by Jesus and associated with the gift of the Spirit. The imagery in such passages as 1 Corinthians 12:13 and Romans 6:3 is tied to birth, washing, putting on clothes, death, and burial. It is always associated with initiation.

- Baptism is a mark of our *inclusion* in the new covenant that Christ established. Through baptism we are "marked" as God's people and the correspondence with circumcision is seen in passages such as Colossians 2:11-12 and 1 Peter 3:20-21. The relationship with circumcision is most disputed by Anabaptists (including Baptist denominations), largely because it supports infant baptism (which they reject). Baptism is performed with water in the name of the Father, Son, and Holy Spirit. Christian baptism symbolises the coming of the Spirit from the Father in the name of the Son. The relationship of water baptism to the gift of the Spirit does vary in the Book of Acts (it is prior to, during, and after water baptism). This simply affirms what Jesus said in John 3:8 about the "mystery" of the working of the Spirit.

- Baptism is a symbol of our *identification* with the death of Christ. This is seen in Romans 6:1-3 and its roots go back to John 19:34-35 where "water and blood" flow from the side of Christ. Baptism and the cross are inextricably linked (see also Matthew 3:14ff and Mark 1:11, where it combines Psalm 2:7 and Isaiah 42:1). Jesus was baptised for the sins of others, and so he was baptised in view of his death. The baptism of water points to the baptism of blood (Luke 12:50; John 19:30; 1 John 5:6) and is rooted in the once-for-all event of Calvary.

- Baptism is a symbol of our *participation* in the resurrected life of Christ. Romans 6:4 emphasises that in Scripture you cannot separate death and resurrection (see Ephesians 2:6; Colossians 3:1). The "new life" is an "ascended life" (Colossians 3:1-4; Romans 6:4).

The pattern of death/resurrection, put off/put on (1 Peter 2:5ff), descent/ascent is to be modelled in our life—death to the "old life" and rising to "newness of life."

• Baptism is a symbol of our *reception* of the Spirit of Christ. This is seen in Jesus's baptism (Matthew 3:16; John 1:32).

• Baptism is an action through which we are *incorporated* into Christ's body. The bestowal of the Spirit, who creates and constitutes the church; we are baptised into this one body (Ephesians 4:4-6).

Baptism of Infants

In the history of Christianity there have been two different traditions regarding the appropriateness of baptism for infant children. We do not know if young children were baptized in the New Testament; however, we are told in the Book of Acts that whole families were baptized upon the conversion of the head of the household (Acts 16:15; 18:8; 1 Corinthians 1:16). Furthermore, we know that in the early centuries, there was widespread practice of infant baptism. A more recent tradition (Anabaptist), influential since the 16th century, has insisted that baptism is for adults only, since only adults are able to understand its implications and exercise saving faith. The Church of the Nazarene, from its beginning days, was composed of persons having roots in both these traditions. Therefore, from our earliest days as a denomination, we have allowed Christian parents to choose whether they will have their babies baptized or opt for the alternative of infant dedication. Our church *Manual* provides rituals for each option. *Infant baptism* expresses the conviction that we are saved by God's grace, which precedes all human action or decision, and that it is only secondarily and consequentially that baptism is a testimony to our human response to God. In infant baptism we bear witness to that truth. When infants are baptized, it is right and necessary that when they come to maturity they make their own confession of faith, and it is possible that they will fail to make such confession. But this cannot be avoided by denying them baptism; otherwise, we would not baptise adult believers either. It becomes, then, the responsibility of the parents and the Church to nurture them, teach them, and guide them toward that eventual confession of personal faith. *Infant dedication* focuses on the human action, not the divine. It tends to rely on a rationalistic understanding of faith rather than a supernatural view of life.

The Question of Re-baptism

According to Michael Green, we seek re-baptism for four main reasons:

1. *Not enough faith because we were too young to understand.* What then of the Jewish covenant (circumcision)? In the New Testament, faith is not the gift, but the "hands" by which we grasp the gift; for an infant, this is the faith of the community.

2. *Not enough confession by the individual.* Yet the church, minister, and parents "confessed."

3. *Not enough water.* Some believe full immersion is the only sign of "burial with Christ," but many traditions believe it is the water itself that is the symbol, not the amount of it.

4. *Not enough feeling.* This is total subjectivism; the need to "feel" baptised.[35]

These reasons are theologically insufficient. God has acted in grace and who are we to deny that? Re-baptism downplays the sacrament as a divine act and focuses on the human act. The covenant is once-for-all; to fall is to need repentance, not to re-do the covenant.

The Sacrament of the Lord's Supper (A Means of Sanctifying Grace)

The institution of the Lord's Supper goes back to Jesus himself and the Last Supper, which was part of the Jewish Passover. There are four key accounts of its institution: Matthew 26:26-30; Mark 14:22-26; Luke 22:14-20; and 1 Corinthians 11:23-26 (against a background of Exodus 24:8-11). The words of institution, "this is my body, this is my blood" are understood in four main ways:

1. Roman Catholic—*transubstantiation.* This view emerges in the 9th century but was made explicit at the IV Lateran Council in

1215. It is the most literal reading of "is." It holds that the outward appearance of bread and wine remain, but the substance is transformed into the literal body and blood of Christ. It focuses on Christ's presence in the elements, and it is a re-presentation of Christ's sacrifice on the altar.

2. Luther—*consubstantiation.* This view seeks to preserve a real presence but holds that the elements remain what they are with Christ present in, with, and under them. The body and blood "come with" the elements; so, it is a real bodily presence based on Luther's view of the ubiquity (omnipresence) of Christ's body.

3. Reformed/Wesleyan—*spiritual presence.* This view holds that the sacraments convey grace through the presence of the Holy Spirit as the elements are faithfully received.

4. Zwingli—*memorial.* This view sees the sacrament as only an external sign; there is no conveyance of grace. The elements signify the body and blood, but there is no actual connection with their physicality. It is a witness to the faith and a reminder of Christ's death.

Images of the Lord's Supper

Based on the language of Scripture, there are various images that help us understand the breadth of the Lord's Supper:

- *Thanksgiving to the Father:* a celebration, a festival, thanksgiving for all God has, is, and will do (Matthew 26:26-30; Mark 14:26-27; Luke 22:14-20; 1 Corinthians 11:23-26; Acts 2:44-46)

- *Commemoration of Christ:* commemoration, memorial, remembrance; "do this in remembrance of me" (Luke 22:19; 1 Corinthians 11:24, cf. v. 25). This is not merely mental recall but entering into the whole story and action (a re-enacting). As such, it encompasses the whole of Creation, Redemption, and Re-Creation.

- *Sacrifice of Ourselves:* the language of the Supper focuses on the on-going reality of the work of Christ as High Priest and Intercessor (Hebrews 7:27; 10:12, 14). We "offer" Christ as our only hope of salvation, and we also offer ourselves (Hebrews 13:15-16) as an act of worship (Romans 6:13; 12:1); in the process, we receive grace.

• *Fellowship of the Faithful:* fellowship, communion (1 Corinthians 10:16, 17). It is an event that binds us together (1 Corinthians 10:19, 20-21; 11:27). We need to remember that none of us are worthy to partake; it is always a gift of grace.

• *Foretaste of Glory:* "until he comes" (1 Corinthians 11:26; Ephesians 1:10). Besides the focus on the death of Christ and Communion as a sombre act (death, sin, costly sacrifice), there is also a focus on the Eschaton (resurrection, banquet of joy, and festivity). This emphasises the presence of Christ as the host of a celebration, the future and coming kingdom; thus, to be celebrated in a festive mood.

For Wesleyans, due to our dynamic view of grace, the Lord's Supper is also a converting ordinance. It is not a reward for worthiness, because all come in need to be graced, not in fitness to be certified. Therefore, it is an open table for all who are drawn by grace and receptive to the Lord's offer of life by the Spirit; all are welcome (Luke 14:7-24; 12:33-35). It is the relationship to God and personal reception that determines the grace received. Wesley increasingly focused on the presence of the Spirit as a Person and our response to his presence, both for healing and increasing awareness of what remains to be healed. The anticipation of the messianic banquet is very strong in Wesley, providing a stimulus for the journey, as well as hope and help for the journey.

QUESTIONS FOR REFLECTION

1. "I only need Jesus and I can worship him at home or out walking on the beach." How would you respond to this opinion?

2. What is your favourite biblical image of the church and why?

3. How would you help your church to understand the importance of the means of grace in spiritual formation?

4. "We do not baptise children because that is what Roman Catholics do." Do you think that is a valid theological position to hold? Why or why not?

5. Do you think it matters how often we celebrate the Lord's Supper? Why or why not?

CHAPTER 10

CONCLUSION

At the heart of the Wesleyan understanding of theology is our relationship with God and then with our neighbour. This is a relationship of love, and it places the focus of the Christian faith on the heart rather than the mind, on trust rather than intellectual comprehension, and on service rather than contemplation. It is not that these elements are unimportant, but that they are secondary to the cultivation of a deep relationship with God and with other people. This keeps Wesleyan theology anchored in ministry instead of philosophical and speculative studies. This focuses our attention on cooperation with others rather than separation over doctrinal differences, if the core affirmations of the ecumenical Creeds are held. Wesleyan theology is concerned to be holistic and tries to always hold together faith and works, the personal and the community, works of piety and works of mercy, the word and the sacraments. In all things, we seek to develop a deeper, transformative relationship with God that genuinely impacts our culture and God's good creation. We believe that it is always God who takes the initiative in establishing a relationship and that the Bible records the long story of his engagement with the human race, with Israel and with the church. It shows us a God of love who has provided all that is needed for the restoration of our relationship with God and, moreover, the renewal of the whole creation.

Such love is not coercive but persuasive and, by prevenient grace, seeks for all to freely respond to his invitation. Such grace enables all who will receive Christ and walk in his ways to be brought into the family of God; none are excluded from God's bounty but by their own choice and rejection of the grace that is freely offered. We believe that all who respond to God's love positively will have a personal assurance of their relationship with him through the ministry of the Holy Spirit. This love is inherently transformative and will lead us to a depth of relationship with God in which his love completely fills the heart, expelling all sin. Such a life is compatible with the reality of our present existence in a fallen body and a fallen world. While faulty understanding, defective judgement, and subsequent imperfect words and actions remain till the Lord returns, they are not freely nor wilfully chosen and therefore do not bring condemnation if freely confessed.

The outcome of this is a passion that every person will come to know God as we know God. The church community not only gathers for worship and the upbuilding of the saints, it also goes out into the streets of its local community to serve the needs of the people and to invite them to experience the love of God. This work of witness is not limited to the immediate neighbourhood, but extends to the uttermost parts of the earth. This is a ministry for the whole church, both lay and clergy, women and men, girls and boys. It is a ministry to the whole person, to every aspect of their lives and their environment. By cooperating with the work of the Holy Spirit, we aim to form faithful, loving people and communities, so that this tradition can be faithfully handed on to the next generation.

Suggestions for Further Reading

Beginner

Abraham, William J. *Wesley for Armchair Theologians.* Louisville: Westminster John Knox, 2005.

LeClerc, Diane. *Discovering Christian Holiness: The Heart of Wesleyan-Holiness Theology.* Kansas City: Beacon Hill Press, 2010.

Thorsen, Don. *An Exploration of Christian Theology.* Peabody: Hendrickson, 2008.

Intermediate to Advanced

Collins, Kenneth J. *The Theology of John Wesley: Holy Love and the Shape of Grace.* Nashville: Abingdon, 2007.

McEwan, David B. *Wesley as a Pastoral Theologian: Theological Methodology in John Wesley's Doctrine of Christian Perfection.* Milton Keynes: Paternoster, 2011.

Maddox, Randy L. *Responsible Grace: John Wesley's Practical Theology.* Nashville: Kingswood/Abingdon, 1994.

Noble, Thomas A. *Holy Trinity, Holy People: The Theology of Christian Perfecting.* Eugene: Cascade Books, 2013.

Staples, Rob L. *Outward Sign and Inward Grace: The Place of the Sacraments in Wesleyan Spirituality.* Kansas City: Beacon Hill Press, 1991.

NOTES

1   *Church of the Nazarene, Manual 2013–2017: History, Constitution, Government, Ritual* (Kansas City: Nazarene Publishing House, 2013), 14-15.

2   Randy Maddox, "John Wesley – Practical Theologian?" *Wesleyan Theological Journal* 23 (1988), 123.

3   *Manual*, 37, emphasis mine.

4   *Manual*, 37.

5   John Wesley, *The Bicentennial Edition of the Works of John Wesley* (Nashville: Abingdon, 1984-), Vol. 11, 310.

6   *Works* 1:225-35, 348-50. See also *Works* 2:439.

7   *Works* 4:355.

8   *Works* 2:475.

9   *Works* 2:475.

10 *Works* 4:295-96.

11 *Works* 2:476.

12 John Wesley, *Explanatory Notes Upon the New Testament*. London: Wesleyan Methodist Book Room, n.d.

13 John Wesley, *The Letters of the Rev. John Wesley*. 8 vols., ed. John Telford (London: Epworth Press, 1931), Vol. 5, 322.

14 See particularly Thomas A. Noble, *Holy Trinity, Holy People: The Theology of Christian Perfecting*. (Eugene: Cascade Books, 2013), 128–57.

15 *Works* 3:203–04.

16 *Works* 2:490.

17 *Works* 13:258–320 and 526–46.

18 See Wesley's sermon, "The Scripture Way of Salvation," *Works* 2:155-69.

19 See Wesley, *Notes on Romans 8:15-16; Galatians 4:5-7*.

20 See Wesley's sermon, "The Great Privilege of Those that are Born of God," *Works* 1:431–43.

21 *Works* 2:160.

22 *Works* 1:264.

23 See Wesley, "The Repentance of Believers," *Works* 1:335–52.

24 *Letters* 3:70.

25 *Works* 3:585.

26 *Letters* 3:167-68.

27 *Letters* 4:213.

28 *Works* 3:422.

29 *Letters* 4:317.

30 *Works* 18:249-50.

31 *Letters* 6:68.

32 C. S. Lewis, *The Problem of Pain* (London: MacMillan, 1976).

33 Thomas A. Noble, "Reflections on Holiness" Paper delivered at the Church of the Nazarene Global Theology Conference, Guatemala, April 2002.

34 *Works* 1:381.

35 Michael Green, *Baptism: Its Purpose, Practice and Power* (Eugene, Oregon: Wipf & Stock, 2010), 113–27.

GLOSSARY

Advent — the arrival of Jesus Christ

amillennialism — See *millennialism*

Anglican — See *Church of England*

apologetics — logical justifications of a doctrine

Apostles' Creed — See *creeds*

apostolicity — related to how authority and authenticity of the Christian faith was passed down from the apostles to our present time

Aquinas — a major theologian and philosopher from Italy who lived in the 13th century. He taught that faith and reason were harmonious.

assize — a high court

Athanasian Creed — See *creeds*

atonement — the doctrine of what it means that "Jesus saves us from sin." The satisfaction theory of atonement holds that Christ suffered and died as a substitute for human sin, thus "satisfying" the justice of God that requires that humans be punished for their sins.

Augsburg Confession — the primary confession of faith of the Lutheran Church. It was a major part of the Protestant

Reformation of the 16th century. See *confession*.

Augustine, Augustinian, Augustinianism — An early theologian and scholar of Christianity, Augustine's teachings heavily influenced orthodox Christianity.

binitarian — a heretical belief that there is one God seen in two persons, usually the Father and Jesus, excluding the Holy Spirit. See *Trinity* and *Unitarian*.

Calvinist — See *Reformed*

canonising — making something authoritative and unchangeable

Cappadocian Fathers — Three theologians of the 4th century (Basil the Great, Gregory of Nyssa, and Gregory of Nazianzus) who taught and developed the doctrine of the Trinity, especially the relationship that exists between the divine Persons of Father, Son, and Holy Spirit.

catholicity — universality

Church of England — The official, established church in England. It is a Protestant church that is known as the Anglican Church outside of England.

confession — formal statements of belief that a particular group holds to be true. Usually, they are based on one or more of the historic creeds of the church. The Church of the Nazarene's confession is the "Articles of Faith" found in the *Manual*. See *Augsburg Confession, Westminster Confession.*

consubstantiation — the Lutheran doctrine that the bread and wine coexist with the body and blood of Christ in substance (but not physically) during the Lord's Supper.

convincing grace — a phrase that Wesley used to speak about the actions of God to bring a person to repentance.

Creed of Constantinople — See *creeds.*

creeds — The historic creeds of the Christian Church come from the first five centuries after the death of Christ. They were the result of the gathering of Christian scholars to resolve divisive questions about theology. There are five major creeds: The Apostles' Creed, which reached its final form around 180 AD; the Nicene Creed, which was written in 325 AD, the Nicene-Constantinopolitan Creed from 381 AD; the Chalcedonian Creed of 451 AD, and the Athanasian Creed of 500 AD.

depravity — the human condition which resulted from sin; the corruption of human nature.

dispensationalism — See *millennialism*

dogma — teachings or principles that are presented as authoritative and completely true

Eastern church; Eastern Orthodox Church — a loose family of churches that branched off from the Roman Catholic Church (known as the Western Church) in 1054 AD. Also called the Orthodox Church.

ecclesiology — the study or doctrine of the Church; that is to say, how we understand the nature of the Church

ecumenical — promoting unity among Christian churches; focusing on common beliefs

elect; election — related to the individuals who receive salvation from God. See *predestination.*

empiricist — someone who believes that all knowledge must be based on experience through the five senses

Enlightenment — an intellectual movement in the 17th and 18th centuries that emphasized reason and individuality rather than tradition

eschatology; eschatological — the study or doctrine of final things, especially death, judgment, the final destiny of the soul

Eschaton — the final event of God's plan for earthly history

final assize — See *assize*

foreordain — to declare that something will happen beforehand. See *predestination.*

Free Church — a church or denomination that is separate from government, usually emphasizing the freedom of the individual to believe or not believe

henotheistic — worshipping or favoring one particular god out of several gods

individualism — the emphasis of each person as self-reliant and independent of the community when it comes to making decisions.

infallible — without the possibility of error

irresistible grace — The Reformed understanding that God will act to save those whom he predestined, overcoming any resistance they may have. One of the five points of Calvinism, commonly listed as the "P" in "T.U.L.I.P."

John Calvin — see *Reformed*

justification — the action of declaring or making someone righteous in God's sight

limited atonement — The Reformed understanding that Jesus' death was only for those whom God predestined for salvation. One of the five points of Calvinism, commonly listed as the "L" in "T.U.L.I.P."

liturgy — a formulary which guides worship

Lutheran — related to the teachings of Martin Luther, the principal figure of the Protestant Reformation of the 16th century. He disputed the Roman Catholic Church's teaching on salvation.

Martin Luther — See *Lutheran*

Methodism, Methodist Church — usually refers to a Protestant denomination, but it also refers to any of the branches of the movement started by John Wesley and others in the 18th century. See *Wesleyan*.

millennial, millennium, millennialism — teachings about the future of humankind as it relates to the thousand-year reign of Christ mentioned in Revelation 20 and marked by the reality of peace justice across the earth. Premillennialism teaches that Christ will return to earth before the 1,000 years. Postmillennialism teaches that Christ will return after the church has effectively evangelized the whole world. Amillenniaism teaches that the 1,000 years are symbolic and that we are already living in God's reign. Dispensationalism is a form of premillennialism that teaches that Christ will return in two stages: the rapture (where believers dead and alive are taken into heaven) followed by a public revelation several years later at which point the 1,000 years will begin.

monotheistic — believing that only one God exists.

Nicene Creed — See *creeds*

orthodox, orthodoxy, orthodox theology — doctrines, theories, and practices that are generally accepted by most Christians. See also *Eastern Church.*

Pauline — related to the teachings of the Apostle Paul.

Pelagian, Pelagianism — related to the teachings of Pelagius, a 4th century theologian who taught that original sin did not taint human nature. That is to say, humans are capable of choosing good or evil without help from God. Augustine opposed this teaching, and it was eventually declared to be a heresy.

perseverance of the saints — The Reformed understanding that those whom God elected to salvation are unable to leave their faith. One of the five points of Calvinism, commonly listed as the "P" in "T.U.L.I.P."

plenary — complete; whole

postmillennialism — See *millennialism*

predestination — the doctrine that God knows or has selected in advance (called "election") those who will be saved.

premillennialism — See *millennialism*

prevenient grace — the actions of God at work in people's lives before they make a decision about salvation. See *preventing grace.*

preventing grace — a phrase that Wesley used to speak about the actions of God that spark hope in the human heart for deliverance from sin and return to God. See *prevenient grace.*

Protestant — related to the Protestant Reformation of the 16th century or to any of the churches that branched from it.

reductionist — someone who tries to describe complex ideas based on its simplest or fundamental parts.

Reformed — related to the teachings and practices of John Calvin and his followers.

reprobate — a calvinistic term describing those whom God did not choose (elect) for salvation

sanctification — the act or process by which someone becomes holy. It means to set apart someone or something for a special purpose.

satisfaction theory of atonement — See *atonement*

soteriology — the study or doctrine of salvation

systematic theology — the reasoned, logical arrangement of beliefs into categories so that they form a consistent whole

Thomas Aquinas — See *Aquinas*

total depravity — The Reformed understanding that all humans are utterly corrupt and sinful because of the fall. One of the five points of Calvinism, commonly listed as the "T" in "T.U.L.I.P." See *depravity.*

transubstantiation — the Roman Catholic doctrine that the bread and wine are converted into the body and blood of Christ in during the Lord's Supper, though they appear unchanged

Trinity, Trinitarian, Triune, Triadic — related to the Christian doctrine of the nature of God, specifically that there exists only one God in three persons: Father, Son, and Holy Spirit

T.U.L.I.P. — The five points of Calvinism that were developed by the followers of John Calvin to oppose the teachings of Jacobus Arminius. The word is formed from the first letters of each of the points: total

depravity, unconditional election, limited atonement, irresistible grace, and preservation of the saints.

unconditional election — The Reformed understanding that God chose ("elected") those who would receive salvation before the world was made. One of the five points of Calvinism, commonly listed as the "U" in "T.U.L.I.P." See *election.*

Unitarian — related to the belief in the complete unity of God and the rejection of the Trinity

universalism — the belief that, eventually, God will save everyone.

Wesleyan; Wesleyanism — related to the teachings of John Wesley, his followers, or the various branches of Methodism (the movement that he and others founded in the 18th century)

Western Church; Western Christianity — usually associated with the Roman Catholic Church or various churches that arose from Western/European society or thought

Westminster Confession — Originally written in 1646, it is the standard confession of the Reformed Church. Other Calvinist churches have used it as the basis for their own doctrinal statements.

FRAMEWORKS FOR LAY LEADERSHIP

ABOUT THE EDITOR

Rob A. Fringer, PhD–Principal and lecturer in Biblical Studies and Biblical Language at Nazarene Theological College in Brisbane. Rob is an ordained elder in the Church of the Nazarene and has 15 years of pastoral experience working in the areas of Youth, Adult Discipleship, and Community Outreach. He is co-author of *Theology of Luck: Fate, Chaos, & Faith* and *The Samaritan Project* both published by Beacon Hill Press of Kansas City. Rob is married (Vanessa) and has two children (Sierra and Brenden).

BOOKS IN THE
FRAMEWORKS FOR LAY LEADERSHIP SERIES

ENGAGING THE STORY OF GOD
Rob A. Fringer

EXPLORING A WESLEYAN THEOLOGY
David B. McEwan

EMBODYING A THEOLOGY OF MINISTRY AND LEADERSHIP
Bruce G. Allder

ENTERING THE MISSION OF GOD
Richard Giesken

EXPRESSING A NAZARENE IDENTITY
Floyd Cunningham

EMBRACING A DOCTRINE OF HOLINESS
David B. McEwan and Rob A. Fringer

www.ingramcontent.com/pod-product-compliance
Lightning Source LLC
Chambersburg PA
CBHW021138020426
42331CB00005B/823